THE EXEMPLUM IN THE EARLY
LITERATURE OF ENGLAND

COLUMBIA
UNIVERSITY PRESS
SALES AGENTS
NEW YORK:
LEMCKE & BUECHNER
30-32 WEST 27TH STREET

LONDON:
HENRY FROWDE
AMEN CORNER, E.C.

TORONTO:
HENRY FROWDE
25 RICHMOND STREET, W.

THE EXEMPLUM IN THE EARLY RELIGIOUS AND DIDACTIC LITERATURE OF ENGLAND

BY

JOSEPH ALBERT MOSHER, Ph.D.

New York

THE COLUMBIA UNIVERSITY PRESS

1911

Copyright, 1911
BY THE COLUMBIA UNIVERSITY PRESS
Printed from type November, 1911

PRESS OF
THE NEW ERA PRINTING COMPANY
LANCASTER, PA.

TO MY MOTHER AND FATHER

This Monograph has been approved by the Department of English in Columbia University as a contribution to knowledge worthy of publication.

A. H. THORNDIKE,

Secretary.

PREFACE

Although the short story in England has been frequently treated, the subject of the present study has hitherto received comparatively slight attention. The exemplum seems never to have assumed in England the importance that it did on the Continent, but my aim has been to show that its part in English life and literature is by no means negligible. Indeed, owing to the various and far-reaching relationships of the type, I have found it inexpedient to carry out my original design to discuss the exemplum in England in all its phases. The field, therefore, still affords opportunities for profitable research which I hope the following pages may in some measure suggest.

In the preparation of the work I have incurred various obligations which are acknowledged with pleasure. For their kind co-operation I desire to thank the librarians of Union Theological Seminary, New York University, and particularly, the librarians and attendants of Columbia University. I am indebted to Professor G. P. Krapp, who proposed the subject, read the manuscript, and offered valuable suggestions; also to Professor H. M. Ayres for reading the manuscript and contributing helpful criticism. My chief obligation is to Professor W. W. Lawrence, who has watched the progress of the work with unfailing interest and has given me the benefit of his accurate and comprehensive knowledge of mediaeval literature.

J. A. M.

Columbia University,
March 9, 1911.

CONTENTS

CHAPTER I

CHAPTER II

CHAPTER III

CHAPTER IV

" If I am not too partial to myself, a variety of anecdote cannot be displeasing to anyone, unless he be morose enough to rival the superciliousness of Cato."

William of Malmesbury,
Gesta Regum Anglorum.

CHAPTER I

The Definition, Origin and Development of the Exemplum

The exemplum may be briefly and conveniently defined as a short narrative used to illustrate or confirm a general statement. But since the term is frequently supposed to comprise a variety of illustrations which do not really belong to the type, it is desirable to consider the definition carefully. To this end we may examine the views of the critics, some representative exempla collections, and the actual use of the type.

Among the critics there appears to be some diversity of opinion upon the subject. Arthur Piaget understands by exempla, " toutes espèces de récits de toutes provenances, empruntés à l'histoire ancienne ou contemporaine, profane ou sacrée, aux vies de saints, aux légendes populaires, aux bestiaires; des anecdotes ou ' faits divers'; tout récit enfin qui, comme le mot l'indique, pouvait servir d'exemple, c'est-à-dire d'éclaircissement ou de preuve à l'appui d'un enseignement moral ou religieux."[1] The inclusion of bestiary material is particularly to be noted. The definition of Gaston Paris includes parables. He says, " Il fut longtemps d'usage d'y [in sermons] introduire ce qu'on appelait des *exemples,* c'est-à-dire, de courts récits, tantôt édifiants en eux-mêmes, tantôt ayant le caractère de paraboles ou même de récits plaisants, desquels le prédicateur extrayait ensuite une moralité."[2] Ten Brink makes especial mention of fables. " The preachers," he says, " and especially the mendicant friars, had long been in the habit of making use of Aesopian fables and other tales in the pulpit."[3] Paul Meyer, however, is of the opinion that the edifying

[1] Petit de Julleville, *Histoire de la Langue et de la Littérature française,* II, 242. The page reference, here, as in all cases, is to the edition cited in the bibliography, where full titles are given.

[2] *La Littérature française au Moyen Age,* 247.

[3] *History of English Literature,* I, 264.

2

1

anecdotes, or supposedly such, called exempla in the Middle Ages, are not to be confused with fables or parables.[4] Thomas Wright mentions among other species of exempla, jests and satirical anecdotes, adaptations from fabliaux, from the metrical poems of the jongleurs, and abridgments of more extensive romances.[5] Professor T. F. Crane states that among the early collectors of illustrations from the sermons of Jacques de Vitry, "sometimes moral reflections, etc., are considered exempla, and sometimes mere references to biographical or historical fact are so treated."[6] Perhaps the most satisfactory classification is that of Lecoy de la Marche. "Les exemples employés par nos [mediaeval French][7] sermonnaires sont de quatre sortes. Les uns sont extraits de l'histoire ou des légendes, particulièrement des historiens de l'antiquité, des chroniques de France, des vies de saints, des livres historiques de la Bible. D'autres sont pris dans les événements contemporains, les anecdotes du domaine publique ou les souvenirs de l'auteur....Les fables composent une troisième catégorie; . . . elle embrasse presque tous les sujets traités par Esope, Phèdre et La Fontaine, plus beaucoup d'autres moins connus. . . . La plupart sont empruntés uniquement au génie populaire, qui les avait enfantés, et à la tradition, qui les avait consacrés; un petit nombre, pourtant, semblent directement puisés chez les écrivains antiques. . . . Le dernier genre d'exemples consiste en descriptions ou en moralités tirées de ces singuliers bestiaires, si communs au moyen âge."[8] In the opinions cited, it is to be observed that while the critics may vary on some points, they uniformly emphasize the narrative element of exempla.

An examination of representative collections shows that the

---

[4] *Romania,* XIV, 390. Cf. also *Les Contes Moralizés de Nicole de Bozon,* introd., v, x.

[5] *Latin Stories,* introd., vi.

[6] *The Exempla of Jacques de Vitry,* introd., xlvii.

[7] It should be remembered that collections of stories circulated freely among the churchmen of all Roman Catholic countries. See J. J. Jusserand, *A Literary History of the English People,* I, 154; also W. J. Courthope, *A History of English Poetry,* I, 152.

[8] *La Chaire française au Moyen Age,* 302–304.

statement of Lecoy de la Marche covers the ground very satisfactorily, although, strictly speaking, bestiary material and fables do not belong to the *genre*. Illustrative passages from bestiaries, lapidaries, and volucriaries are by no means wanting in the religious and moral literature of the Middle Ages; they are, like fables, sometimes even designated by the term "bysen," "ensampel," or "exemplum." But it is to be noted that illustrations from nature are rarely found in the standard collections of exempla, and that they are altogether lacking in the most notable storehouses, such as the *Dialogues* of Gregory, the *Disciplina Clericalis* of Petrus Alphonsus, the *Factorum et Dictorum memorabilium* of Valerius Maximus, the *Dialogus Miraculorum* of Caesar of Heisterbach, and the *Tractatus de diversis materiis praedicabilibus* of Étienne de Bourbon. Moreover, where bestiary and kindred matter does appear, it is usually distinguished from the narratives. A notable case in point is the *Contes Moralizés* of Nicole de Bozon, where the essential part of the work consists of statements about the nature or "property" of plants, animals or stones, followed by moralizations drawn from them. For illustrating the moral so drawn, tales are added, under the caption "Narratio ad Idem" or "Fabula ad Idem," entirely distinct from the "properties of things" and the moralizations. Another work in which the distinction is felt if not openly indicated is Robert Holkot's *Liber Sapientiae,* where passages from natural history are jumbled together with narratives, analogies, metaphors, similes and moralizings. In such a case there seems to be no more reason for calling a bestiary passage an exemplum than for so designating a simile or metaphor. Certainly figures of speech should be excluded from the exemplum class, although "bysen," "ensampel" and "exemplum" are frequently applied to them. The following passages from the works of English writers will indicate the varied application of these terms to figures of speech.

In Alfred's *Boethius,* Mind has asked Philosophy to show what true happiness is; Philosophy replies, "Ic wille forlustlice for þinum lufum; ac ic sceal be sumre bysene sume anlicnesse

þære wisan þe getæcan, oþþe þæt þing cuþre sie."[9] The
examples cited are to the effect that whoever would sow fertile
land must first pluck up all the weeds so that the wheat may
grow better; that everybody thinketh honey-comb the sweeter
after tasting something bitter; that calm weather is more
delectable after a storm, day after night; so, happiness after
misery. In the same work Alfred calls the well-known comparison of godly and careless men with the parts of a wheel,
a "bispell."[10]

In the homily on the Nativity of our Lord, Aelfric uses the
term "bysen" in reference to an analogy. Speaking of the
divine and human nature of Christ, which is neither mingled
nor yet separated, he says: "We mihton eow secgan ane lytle
bysne, gif hit to waclic nære; Sceawa nu on anum æge, hu
þæt hwite ne biþ gemenged to þam geolcan, and biþ hwæþere
an æg. Nis eac Cristes godcundnys gerunnen to þære menni-
scnysse, ac he þurhwunaþ þeah a on ecnysse on anum hade
untotwæmed."[11]

Wulfstan uses similar examples. For instance, in "Lar-
spell" (No. xlix), after stating that those who seek to raise
themselves to high positions are most liable to be stricken down,
he says, "Swa we magon be þam þa bysne oncnawan and
ongitan, þæt treow þonne, þe wexeþ on þam wudubearwe, þæt
hit hlifaþ up ofer eall þa oþre treowu and brædeþ hit, þonne
semninga storm gestandeþ and se stranga wind, þonne biþ hit
swiþlicor geweged and geswencged, þonne se oþer wudu."[12]

In the *Old English Homilies,* the writer says with reference
to fasting, that the sinner fasts to cleanse himself from sin, the
righteous man to preserve his righteousness and approach holiness, and the holy man to exalt his seat in heaven; then he
adds, "and þis us doþ to understonden þe forbisne of þe was-
shestren." This "forbisen" tells how some bear soiled clothes
to the water for washing—so fasteth the sinful man to be
cleansed of his foul sins; others bear clean clothes to the water

[9] *King Alfred's Old English Version of Boethius,* 51.
[10] *Ibid.,* 129.
[11] Aelfric's *Homilies,* I, 40; see also pp. 212, 286, 304.
[12] *Wulfstan Homilies,* 262.

to be bleached—so doth the righteous man to please our Lord and to have eternal life, etc.[13]

The author of the *Ancren Riwle* introduces a comparison between a castle surrounded by a filled moat and a man sur-rounded by the ditch of humility, with the expression " another example."[14] In the Second Sunday Sermon of the *English Metrical Homilies,* the Biblical comparison concerning the budding fig tree and the signs of the approach of the heavenly kingdom is called an " ensampel."[15] Another writer who uses the term " example " with reference to a figure of speech is the author of the Middle English dialogue, *Vices and Virtues,* written about 1200. He refers to Saint Gregory as the source of the example (forbisen) that just as no web can be woven without two beams, so charity can never be accomplished with-out two loves, God's and man's.[16]

Richard Rolle's treatises abound in similes such as the one that just as the lords of castles send help to the besieged, so God sends help to those who are troubled in their souls. Opposite this figure the word " exemplum "[17] is written in the margin of the manuscript. Similar instances are frequent.[18] The reli-gious treatise, *Jacob's Well,* composed during the first quarter of the fifteenth century, has the same marginal note " exem-plum " or " exemplum bonum " opposite some of its figures of speech.[19]

These instances show that the term " example " was pretty generally applied to figures of speech and analogies, even after the exemplum had become a well-defined form in religious and didactic literature. It is quite likely that some writers con-sidered any illustration whatever an exemplum. Others, per-haps recognizing a distinction between an example and an

---

[13] *Old English Homilies,* Second Series, 57 ; see also First Series, 80.

[14] *Ancren Riwle,* 247.

[15] *English Metrical Homilies,* 22.

[16] *Vices and Virtues,* 38.

[17] *Richard Rolle and his Followers,* II, 47.

[18] *Ibid.,* I, 134, 138, 143.

[19] *Jacob's Well,* 178.

exemplum, may have carelessly confused the two at times.[20]
There is strong probability that in the great majority of cases,
the word " example " when used with reference to bestiary passages, figures of speech, moralizations and analogies, was used
in the general sense of an illustration and not in the restricted
sense of an exemplum,[21] which grew up in the Roman Church
as a distinct species of illustration based upon actual or
supposedly actual happenings.[22]

To sum up, there seems to be warrant for limiting the
application of the term "exemplum" inasmuch as (1) the
grounds on which the critics agree, (2) the great body of
collections, (3) the vast number of instances where the term
is obviously used in a technical sense, and (4) the fundamental
idea of basing the illustration on human experience, clearly
indicate that the essentials of an exemplum are: (1) a brief
narrative; (2) human characters. Fables, since they were frequently considered as exempla by mediaeval collectors and
preachers, cannot be ignored in the following study, but such
illustrations as figures of speech, analogies, bestiary and lapi-
dary passages, will receive only incidental consideration.

In spite of the elimination of kindred forms, it has already
been made apparent that the material for exempla is of vast
amount. An examination of the field shows that the sources
from which exempla were taken may be divided into four
classes: (1) such incidental material as was afforded by historical works, secular and ecclesiastical; poems and prose
fiction, ancient and mediaeval; contemporary events; incidents
and stories brought personally to the attention of the writer;
(2) collections of tales, fables, anecdotes, and saints' lives, not

---

[20] Such a confusion would account for the fact that among the early
collectors from the sermons of Jacques de Vitry, " Sometimes moral reflections, etc.," are considered exempla. See above, p. 2.

[21] Cf. the word "character," and the term "characters" associated with
Hall, Overbury and others.

[22] The exemplum was established by Gregory the Great on the ground that
to acquaint people with actual experiences of men was often more efficacious
than to employ precept only. Jacques de Vitry, the Knight of La Tour
Landry and other influential writers, considered the exemplum in the
same light. See below, pp. 13, 14.

originally designed to serve as exempla but offering plentiful
and convenient matter for such; these are represented respectively by the numerous early collections of Latin stories,
Aesopic fable collections, the historical anecdotes of Valerius
Maximus, and the *Legenda Aurea* of Jacobus de Voragine;
(3) elaborate moral and didactic treatises which make use of a
large number of exempla in illustration of the points discussed;
to this class belong the *Dialogues* of Gregory, the *Disciplina
Clericalis* of Petrus Alphonsus, and *Jacob's Well*; (4) collections especially designed for the use of preachers and moralists
and properly designated as "example-books"; of this class
there are four varieties: (*a*) collections containing exempla
unclassified and without accompanying moralizations, such as
the early compilations from the sermons of Jacques de Vitry;
(*b*) collections containing exempla classified under topics
alphabetically but without moralizations, such as the *Alphabetum Narrationum* formerly ascribed to Étienne de Besançon;
(*c*) collections containing exempla moralized but not classified,
such as the *Gesta Romanorum;* (*d*) collections containing
exempla both alphabetically classified and moralized, such as
the *Scala Celi* of Johannes Junior.

These example-books, although differing from one another
in the number and length of the tales, show great similarity in
manner and matter. This is accounted for by the substantial
unity of purpose on the part of the collectors. An unelaborated
outline which set forth the moral unmistakably and could be
developed at the discretion of the preacher or moralist was
considered the most advantageous form for exempla in the
collections. In style, therefore, a dead level prevails. As to
subject-matter, stories concerning good and bad bishops, monks,
friars and hermits preponderate; incidents from the lives of
saints are next in general favor; fables constitute the third
choice. Copious borrowing from a few well-known early storehouses, such as the *Vitae Patrum,* Gregory's *Dialogues,* the
Dialogus Miraculorum of Caesar of Heisterbach, the *Factorum
et Dictorum memorabilium* of Valerius Maximus, saints' lives,
and Aesopic fables, naturally resulted in much repetition.
Constant copying and recopying of favorite and effective

stories tended to preserve the similarity. A glance at the notes of any well-edited collection, such as Professor Crane's *Jacques de Vitry,* will indicate what a large number of tales were repeated again and again in European collections. Variant forms, of course, abound, and as new material of a literary or historical character developed, new stories were added here and there; but the old favorites and the same general tone of the collections survived through the entire flourishing period of the exemplum.

This vast amount of diversified material, which the assiduity of collectors placed at the disposal of moralists and preachers, afforded tales suitable for widely varying audiences and occasions. There were tales for the serious and the frivolous, for the sinful and the godly, for the churchman and the layman. The purposes served by exempla may be summed up as follows: (1) to furnish a concrete illustration of the result of obeying or disobeying some religious or moral law; (2) to give proof or confirmation of the truth of an assertion; (3) to arouse fear in the sinful or to stimulate the zeal of the godly; (4) to make clear the meaning of some abstruse statement; (5) to revive languid listeners, evoke interest or laughter; (6) to eke out a scant sermon by "farsing" it with tales. The last two of these purposes were emphasized by men like Chaucer's Pardoner, who contributed largely to bring the exemplum into disrepute. They may all be found in varying proportion in sermons and treatises from the time of Gregory the Great onward.

Having in mind the nature of the exemplum, the character of the sources, and the purposes served by the type, we may proceed to a brief discussion of its origin and development in European literature. This has been presented, with particular emphasis on collections, by T. F. Crane,[23] and discussed incidentally by numerous other critics, such as Warton, Dunlop, Douce, Wright, Herrtage, Furnivall, Jacobs, Ten Brink, Goedke, Cruel, Horstmann, Aubertin, Gaston Paris, Lecoy de la Marche, Heaureau, Bourgain and Hervieux.[24] To these men

[23] T. F. Crane, *The Exempla of Jacques de Vitry;* see introd.
[24] See bibliography at the close of this study.

and others I am considerably indebted for the material in the following section, which aims to afford a convenient view of the rise and decline of the exemplum.

The value of the apologue, the concrete illustration, was perceived by the greatest of teachers, Christ. His use of the parable, such as that of the Sower, the Talents, or the Prodigal Son, was his favorite means of instruction. In the use of apologues, however, Christ was not an originator, inasmuch as this method of inculcating morals was popular in the East before Christianity was ever conceived. Such Eastern collections as the *Book of Sindibad (Seven Sages)*, the *Fables of Bidpai (Kalilah and Dimnah)*, the *Bhagavan Bodhisattvascha (Barlaam and Josaphat)*, and the *Vedabbha Jataka (Buddhist Birth Stories)*, show that the illustrative tale must have been favored by the moralists of antiquity.

It is not improbable that such usage arose independently among various peoples. That it should be imitated after proving effective was altogether natural. " Greece and India," says Joseph Jacobs, " each invented separately the fable as a means of moral or political instruction. Similarly Judea and India, each probably independently, invented the parable for the same purpose. Both the Rabbis and the Brahmins found that the best way to point a moral was to adorn a tale. Both Jesus and Buddha adopted the method of their rivals for the purpose of their propaganda."[25]

It was a long time before these oriental collections were introduced into Europe. In fact, the earliest known western compilation of oriental apologues, the *Disciplina Clericalis* of Petrus Alphonsus, was not made until the beginning of the twelfth century.[26] Nor was the method of teaching by apologues,[27]

[25] *Barlaam and Josaphat*, introd., lv–lvi.

[26] Cf. T. F. Crane, *Mediaeval Sermon-Books and Stories, Amer. Philosophical Society Publications*, XXI, 50, note.

[27] The part later played by oriental tales is emphasized by Gaston Paris. " D'ou venaient ces contes, répandus dans toute l'Europe, et dont plusieurs sont populaires encore aujourd'hui ? La plupart avaient une origine orientale . . . le bouddhisme, ami des exemples et des paraboles, contribua à faire recueillir des contes de toutes parts et en fit aussi inventer d'excellents." *La Littérature française au Moyen Age*, 119.

which had been effectively used by the Brahmins, Nestorians, Rabbins, and finally by Christ, extensively adopted by the Christian teachers of the early period. This fact may, perhaps, be accounted for by the extreme vogue of the symbolical method, the explanation of Scripture according to its moral, historical or spiritual significance.[28]   The sermons of Augustine, Jerome, and Gregory the Great are replete with exegesis of this kind, and their influence in this respect is one of the remarkable features of mediaeval literature.[29]   The last of these men did, however, recognize the value of the narrative illustration, and established in homiletic literature the formal exemplum, which was evolved from the Eastern apologue and parable.   Thirteen exempla, dealing almost exclusively with incidents concerning clerics, are to be found in Gregory's forty *Homiliae in Evangelia,*[30] which are of a comparatively popular nature.   Eight of the tales are taken from Gregory's own compilation, the *Dialogues.*[31]   Besides the fully developed exempla, there are in these homilies many brief references used to confirm or illustrate doctrine.

Gregory's belief in the efficacy of exempla is evinced not only by his employment of them, but by commendatory statements.   In one place he says, " Sed quia nonnunquam mentes audientium plus exempla fidelium quam docentium verba convertunt, volo vobis aliquid de proximo dicere, quod corda vestra tanto formidolosius audiant, quanto eis hoc de propinquo

[28] " The allegorical interpretation, first introduced by Philo as a means to reconcile the Mosaic revelation with the Greek philosophy, was adopted by the Alexandrian theologians as the highest principle of Biblical exegesis, and through St. Augustine transplanted to the Western Church. In the Middle Ages four senses were found in Scripture: historical, allegorical, moral, and anagogical; e. g.: Jerusalem is literally the city so named, allegorically the Church, morally the believing soul, anagogically the heavenly Jerusalem." See Horstmann, *Richard Rolle of Hampole,* I, introd., ix; see also Harnack, *Hist. of Dogma,* I, 114 seq.

[29] In the writings of the great Fathers of the Latin Church " are to be found those myriad mystical allegorical interpretations of Scripture which were to dominate the literature and inspire the art of the Middle Ages." H. O. Taylor, *The Classical Heritage,* 104.

[30] Edited by Migne, *Patrologia Latina,* LXXVI.

[31] Edited by Migne, *Patr. Lat.,* LXXVII.

sonat."[32] Again he states that "ad amorem Dei et proximi plerumque corda audientium plus exempla quam verba excitant."[33] These statements were employed later by a number of men who quote from Gregory to justify the method.[34] Furthermore, Gregory gave still greater encouragement to the use of the type by his compilation of the *Dialogues,* already mentioned. This work, as may be remembered, consists of a conversation between Gregory and his deacon Peter. The former tells tales, after which the latter asks questions in such a way as to bring out the moral points involved and lead to other tales. The first section relates incidents from the lives of Constantine, Boniface, Fortunatus, Severus and others; the second deals with Saint Benedict; the third and fourth narrate wonders concerning various holy men. The book was probably composed in emulation of the *Vitae Patrum,* with the idea of comparing the miracles of the Latin hermits with those of the Egyptians.[35] In the prologue, Gregory states that the narratives were principally intended to lead men to better lives; for this purpose, exempla were, in his opinion, often more efficacious than ordinary exposition of Scripture: "Sunt nonnulli, quos ad amorem patriae coelestis plus exempla, quam praedicamenta succendunt."[36] The influence of the *Dialogues* on the later development of exempla can hardly be overestimated, inasmuch as nearly every important collector after Gregory drew copiously from it. In three ways, therefore, this great churchman encouraged the use of exempla: by employing them in his homilies; by recommending their efficacy; and by writing a treatise which was, to all intents and purposes, a collection of exempla.

[32] *Homiliae, Patr. Lat.,* LXXVI, 1290. Professor Crane points out that Gregory here refers to the examples of men themselves, but the fact that the homilist says that he therefore wishes to tell of a recent happening would seem to indicate that the exemplum was not far from his mind. This is one of the passages frequently cited by later users of exempla. See Crane, *J. de V.,* introd., xviii.

[33] *Homiliae, Patr. Lat.,* LXXVI, 1300.

[34] Jacques de Vitry; Étienne de Bourbon; the author of the *Alphabetum Narrationum* (Arnold of Liège?); the author of the anonymous *Speculum Exemplorum.*

[35] Gaston Paris, *La Littérature française, 232.*

[36] *Dialogues,* Migne, *Patr. Lat.,* LXXVII, 153.

Gregory's encouragement did not, however, result in much employment of the type.[37] Not until about the time of the preaching friars did it become a marked feature in European sermons. Still, as will be seen later, exempla circulated in Latin among the churchmen before being extensively used in popular discourses.[38] Some anecdotes and legends appear in French sermons of the twelfth century,[39] and they were not altogether wanting in contemporary German preaching.[40] But in the main, the evidence leads to the conclusion that the exemplum was comparatively little employed before the opening of the thirteenth century. Wright says, "The preachers of the thirteenth, fourteenth and fifteenth centuries, attempted to illustrate their texts and to inculcate their doctrines, by fables and stories."[41] Gaston Paris notes that stories were inserted in sermons after the twelfth century.[42] Aubertin, speaking of the fourteenth century, says that then, as in the thirteenth, there was "emploi fréquent des exemples, recommandé par les rhétoriques sacrées et justifié par des succès éclatants."[43] Paul Meyer states that either exempla were not of frequent occurrence up to the thirteenth century, or that the sermons of a popular character where they would naturally be found, have not been preserved.[44] Lecoy de la Marche, who has made a particularly careful study of French sermons, says, "Les exemples proprement dits sont rares avant le XIIIᵉ siècle."[45] The above statements seem to show pretty conclusively that previous to the beginning of the thirteenth century, the use of exempla was slight.

[37] Crane, *J. de V.*, introd., xviii.

[38] Cf. M. B. Heaureau, "*Les Récits d'Apparitions,*" printed in *Mémoires de l'Institut national de France*, XXVIII, Pt. II, 261.

[39] See Bourgain, *La Chaire française au XIIe Siècle*, 258 seq.

[40] See R. Cruel, *Geschichte der deutschen Predigt im Mittelalter*, Chap. III.

[41] *Latin Stories*, introd., vi.

[42] *La Littérature française*, 120.

[43] *Histoire de la Langue et de la Littérature françaises au Moyen Age*, II, 358.

[44] *Les Contes Moralizés*, introd., xi.

[45] *La Chaire française*, 299.

From the time of Cardinal Jacques de Vitry and the preaching friars, the exemplum rapidly became a prominent element
of sermons. This was due largely to the fact that these men
began an appeal to the masses. For this purpose, cold, pedantic
arguments and scholastic subtleties were futile;[46] the people
must be interested. The far-sighted and influential churchman,
Jacques de Vitry, like the Franciscans and Dominicans,
realized the necessity and stated it clearly. In the prologue to
his *Sermones Vulgares* he says that the keen sword of subtle
argumentation has no power over laymen; that to the knowledge of the Scriptures, without which one cannot take a step,
must be added exempla which are encouraging, amusing, and
yet edifying.[47] Other men who collected or used illustrative
material stated their approval of the exemplum as an effective
factor in discourse. Some of the more important of these may
be cited here.

Odo de Ceritona, who flourished in England during the last
quarter of the twelfth century, wrote in the prologue to his
Parabolae, " Et quoniam, ut dicit Gregorius, plus quandoque
compungunt exempla quam verba, aperiam in parabolis os
meum, et similitudines et exempla que libencius audiuntur,
memorie firmius quam verba commendantur, proponam, quibus
intellectis sapiens sapiencior erit."[48]

Étienne de Bourbon in the prologue to his *Tractatus de
diversis materiis praedicabilibus* states that his object is to stir
men to eschew vain worldly delights and to seek eternal good;
he then adds a recommendation of exempla, citing Gregory,
Christ and Dionysius in support of his views.[49] The prologue
closes with another authoritative commendation of exempla

[46] Caesar of Heisterbach in his *Dialogus Miraculorum* says, " When I
speak of God you sleep, but to listen to fables you rouse yourselves." See
Histoire littéraire de la France, XXIV, 381.

[47] See Crane, *J. de V.,* introd., xli–xlii, note.

[48] See Hervieux, *Les Fabulistes Latins,* IV, 175. Earlier in the prologue Odo says, " Paterfamilias debet proferre de thesauro suo nova et
vetera verba et exempla, quibus reficiatur fidelis anima."

[49] See Lecoy de la Marche, *Anecdotes historiques,* 4.

taken from the thirteenth century *Life of St. Dominic* by Bishop Constantin of Orvieto.[50]

The author of the *Alphabetum Narrationum,* formerly ascribed to Étienne de Besançon, cites in his prologue the authority of Gregory and St. Dominic and adds at considerable length his own recommendation of exempla as a means of instilling morality. "Narrationes quidem hujus (modi) et exempla facilius intellectu capiuntur, et memoriae firmius imprimuntur, et a multis libentius audiuntur."[51]

At a later period the Knight of La Tour Landry, among others, is a firm believer in the moral benefits of exempla. In the introduction to his book of stories compiled for the instruction of his daughters, he says that the work was done "affin que elles peussent aprendre et estudier, et veoir et le bien et la mal qui passé est, pour elles garder de cellui temps qui à venir est."[52] Other references might be added to show that the collectors felt that they were greatly advancing the cause of religion and morality by their work.[53]

Both collectors and preachers were encouraged by the writers of treatises on the art of preaching, to gather and employ exempla. A few cases in point may be mentioned. Alanus de Insulis, who died about 1203, advises in his *Summa de Arte Praedicatoria* that authorities should be cited, quotations inserted, also "verba commotiva, quae mentes emolliant, et lacrymas pariant." He then adds, "In fine vero, debet uti exemplis, ad probandum quod intendit, quis familiaris est

---

[50] "'Ubicunque conversabatur beatus Dominicus, sive in via cum sociis, aut in domo cum hospite reliquaque familia, aut inter magnates et principes vel prelatos, semper effluebat edificatoriis sermonibus, habundabat exemplis, quibus ad amorem Christi seculive contemptum audiencium animos invitabat; et vix ipsa communis ejus locucio a virtutis pondere vacua erat.'" *Anecdotes historiques,* 13; for corrected form of the passage, see editor's note, *ibid.,* 14.

[51] See *Hist. litt. de la France,* XX, 273. An early English translation of *Alphabetum,* entitled *An Alphabet of Tales,* is in process of edition by Mrs. M. M. Banks for the E. E. T. S. Under the heading "Exemplum," the compiler gives further evidence of the efficacy of tales; see *Alphabet,* Pt. I, 217.

[52] La Tour Landry, *Le Livre,* 3–4.

[53] See Crane, *J. de V.,* introd., xx–xxi.

doctrina exemplaris."[54] An anonymous work of the thirteenth century, entitled *De Dilatione Sermonum,* points out the various steps by which a sermon should be developed. The third step is the reasoning or argumentation, which may consist in bringing forth two contrary propositions with the idea of rejecting one of them; in linking enthymemes; or in narrating exempla.[55] Humbert de Romans, who in the latter part of the thirteenth century had considerable influence over the Dominicans and Franciscans, also recommended the use of exempla, in his *De Eruditione Praedicantium.*[56] These citations may suffice to indicate that from the beginning of the thirteenth century the use of exempla was advocated by instructors in theology.

The vogue of exempla spread rapidly all over western Europe. In France, Germany, Italy, Spain and England, were produced a number of sermon collections, usually entitled "Sermones de tempore et de sanctis," in which exempla were employed. Often the collector added an appendix consisting of tales, which was known as a "promptuarium." The sources of the tales in these collections were widespread and various, but those most frequently quoted were the *Vitae Patrum,* the *Dialogues* of Gregory, the *Dialogus Miraculorum* of Caesar of Heisterbach, the *Factorum et Dictorum memorabilium* of Valerius Maximus, and saints' lives.

The immediate success of exempla in the popular sermons of the preaching friars, gave rise to a large demand for more example-books. They were soon produced in large numbers. The more important works, such as those of Jacques de Vitry, Étienne de Bourbon, Vincent de Beauvais, and the author of the *Alphabetum Exemplorum,* were scattered over Europe in copies and excerpts, and new compilations were made. The standard sources continued to furnish the most favored stories, many of which became so familiar that often only a few opening words of them were given in the collections. Up to the middle of the fourteenth century, collections had appeared in which the tales were accompanied by moralizations; also those

[54] *Summa,* Migne, *Patr. Lat.,* CCX, 114.
[55] *La Chaire française,* 296.
[56] *Ibid.,* 301.

in which the tales were alphabetically arranged. About the middle of the century, a writer styling himself "Frater Johannes Junior, ordinis fratrum predicatorium," compiled a work called the *Scala Celi* in which there were both alphabetical arrangement of the stories under topical headings, and frequent moralizations of the tales. The plan of this book represents the final stage in the development of example-books. The work of the preacher was reduced to a minimum.

The ease with which sermons could be prepared by employing these plentifully distributed tales, and the satisfaction of the great mass of auditors in hearing them, resulted in excessive use of the type. There was, moreover, a marked tendency in favor of indelicate and even vicious narratives.[57] As a consequence, opposition to exempla was aroused and by the time of Dante became outspoken. The great Florentine expressed in his *Paradiso* a feeling of strong resentment at the excessive use of tales and fables in the sermons of his day.

> " . . . e'en they whose office is
> To preach the gospel, let the gospel sleep,
> And pass their own inventions off instead.
> One tells how at Christ's suffering the wan moon
> Bent back her steps, and shadow'd o'er the sun
> With intervenient disk, as she withdrew;
> Another, how the light shrouded itself
> Within its tabernacle, and left dark
> The Spaniard and the Indian, with the Jew.
> Such fables Florence in her pulpit hears,
> Bandied about more frequent than the names
> Of Bindi and of Lapi in her streets.
> . . . .
> The preacher now provides himself with store
> Of jests and jibes; and, so there be no lack
> Of laughter, while he vents them his big cowl
> Distends, and he has won the meed he sought."[58]

Similar objection to the use of tales and fables in sermons was not uncommon. Professor Schofield calls attention to the words of the thirteenth century French preacher, Gautier de

[57] "The most scandalous tales were not considered out of place by the preachers of the thirteenth century." Robinson, *Petrarch*, 92–93.

[58] *Paradiso*, Canto XXIX, ll. 99 seq., Cary's translation.

Chateau-Thierry, relative to John's sending the disciples to Christ: "'Audiebat verba oris eius, non opera regum, vel Renardi, vel fabulas.'"[59] In England, as in Italy and France, we find the same criticism. Perhaps the most vigorous opponent of story-telling in the pulpit was John Wycliffe, whose sermons and tracts contain numerous passages directed against the employment of narratives. For example, in the tract "Of the Leaven of Pharisees," written about 1381, he deplores the fact that the friars "maken hem besi on þe holy day to preche fablis and lesyngis to þe peple and not þe gospel, and gon fro place to place and fro man to man to begge of pore men for here false lesyngis, and letten men fro here devocioun."[60] Again, he says, "þei techen opynly fablys, cronyklis and lesyngis and leven cristis gospel and þe maundementis of god."[61] In another place he states that these friars "han disceyved cristendom þis hundred ȝeer & more bi ypocrisie & false prechynge of fablis & errouris & heresies."[62] In the tract "Of Prelates" Wycliffe states that "þei senden oþere þat tellen lesyngis, fablis, & cronyclis, & robben þe peple bi fals beggyngis."[63] Similar references from the work of Wycliffe and his followers might be multiplied, in which "iapis," "gabbyngis," "lesyngis," "cronyclis," "fablis," "tradicions," and "poisies" are decried.[64] At a later period we find that criticism of the use of exempla is still alive. For instance, Erasmus in his *Concionator* deprecates the exemplum;[65] and as Douce points out, ridicules in his *Stultitiae Laus*, the story-

---

[59] W. H. Schofield, *English Literature from the Norman Conquest to Chaucer*, 342.

[60] *The English Works of Wycliffe*, 8.

[61] *Ibid.*, 16; see also p. 10.

[62] *Ibid.*, 26.

[63] *Ibid.*, 59.

[64] *Ibid.*, 105, 124, 144, 153, 305–6, 310, 347, 438, 442, 468, 469.

[65] *Ecclesiastae sive de ratione concionandi*, 529. "Ab exemplis fabulosis, quamquam et his ratione quadam utuntur oratores, ecclesiastae in totum abstinendum censeo, duntaxat apud promiscuam multitudinem. Video quidem fuisse morem nostra memoria, ut concionatores narrationibus quibusdam uterentur sub rationis finem, quae videri poterant studio confictae ad terrorem incutiendum rudibus et obduratis, aut ut rem alioqui frugiferam persuaderent."

3

telling theologians.[66] Along with these individual outcries against the use of tales, more formidable opposition had appeared: the Church Councils had joined issue with exempla.

The action of the Councils was not taken, apparently, until the Catholic Reaction had set in and it had long been felt that exempla were exercising a pernicious influence. Toward the close of the fourteenth century a strong official sentiment against the type existed, though actual prohibition was yet deferred. In the Council of Salzburg (1386) it was maintained that "'These false prophets [the wandering friars] by their sermons full of fables often lead astray the souls of their hearers.'"[67] More definite action was taken considerably later. At the Council of Sens (1528), the first Council of Milan (1565), and the Council of Burgos (1624), measures were finally enacted to exclude the objectionable narratives.[68] The exemplum at this time had passed through its flourishing period, but still the Councils were unable to make their rulings immediately effective.

The number of collections compiled, however, is comparatively small after the fifteenth century. A few voluminous works belong to the latter half of the sixteenth and the opening of the seventeenth centuries. In 1555, John Herold, a scholar and editor of Basel, published his great three-volume collection entitled *Exempla virtutum et vitiorum, atque etiam aliarum rerum maxime memorabilium, future lectori supra modum magnus thesaurus.* A similar work, the *Promptuarium Exem-*

---

[66] Douce, *Illustrations of Shakspere,* II, 343. The passage referred to, runs as follows: "Hic mihi stultam aliquam et indoctam fabulam, ex speculo opinor historiali, aut Gestis Romanorum, in medium adferunt, et eandem interpretantur allegoricè, tropologicè, et anagogicè." *Stultitiae Laus,* 261. Douce further states (p. 343) that the Italians had not entirely ceased using exempla even in the eighteenth century. "Grossley," he continues, "states that he heard a buffoon preacher at Rome who stuffed his discourse with a thousand tales, among which was that of Father Philip's geese, from Boccaccio." Barclay in *The Ship of Fools* says that priests and clerks who tell gestes of Robin Hood in the pulpit are doubtless fools before God, if not before man. Cf. Snell, *Age of Transition,* I, 127–28.

[67] See J. J. Jusserand, *English Wayfaring Life,* 303.

[68] See Crane, *J. de V.,* introd., lxix–lxx.

plorum of Andreas Hondorrf, a German Lutheran minister, was published in 1580. In 1603, Johannes Major, a Jesuit of Douay, revised and added to the enormous anonymous collection called the *Speculum Exemplorum.*[69] Other collections, such as the *Exempla virtutum et vitiorum* of Giovanni Vittoria Rossi, are even later. But the Reformation had brought exempla into general disrepute and they had long since become associated with *facetiae,* jests and secular tales.

[69] An edition of this revision, the *Magnum Speculum Exemplorum,* as late as 1718 is noted. Crane, *J. de V.,* introd., lxxv.

CHAPTER II

The Exemplum in English before the Coming of the Friars

The remarkable and sudden popularity of exempla in western Europe from the beginning of the thirteenth century has over-shadowed the earlier appearance of the type, especially in English literature.[1] Its employment here was, indeed, relatively small, and does not seem to continue in unbroken connection with the later period. But as may be inferred from the preceding chapter, the exemplum, owing to its detachment and simplicity, might easily be in vogue for a time, fall into disuse, and be revived without changing its essential form. It is not surprising that the use of the type in the early period dies out and leaves little trace upon English literature. The exemplum in Old English is, nevertheless, worthy of consideration.

It is interesting to find that it makes its first appearance in England through Gregory the Great, who by precept, by the compilation of the *Dialogues,* and by a more or less systematic employment in his homilies, stood as a sponsor for the type. His *Pastoral Care,* translated by Alfred and sent "to every bishopric in my kingdom," marks the beginning of the use of exempla in English literature. The illustrations in this work are very different in subject-matter from the monkish tales which are usually thought of in connection with the term "exempla." They lack, moreover, the detachment, stock introductions and conclusions, and position at the close of sections, characteristic of the type at a later period. Still, they are narrative passages used consciously to illustrate the doctrines of the text. In a few cases the incidents are introduced by statements which suggest that they were more or less clearly recognized as exempla. For instance, the account of David

---

[1] The subject has been briefly touched upon by H. S. Canby in *The Short Story in England,* pp. 24 seq.

cutting a piece from Saul's cloak instead of killing him, begins, "Ac gif we nu onginnaþ reccean ongemong þisum ymbe Davides dæda sume, þonne magon we þis spell þy openlicor gereccean."[2] The introduction to the episode of Abner and Asahel runs, "Þæt we magon openlicor gecyþan, gif we Abneres dæda sume herongemong sæcgeaþ, hu Assael hiene unwærlice mid anwalde þreatode, & him oferfylgde."[3] In another place the writer, referring to the devil's use of flattery to soothe a disconsolate sinner, says, "Þæt wæs mid þære biesene getacnod þe Dinan gedon wæs Iacobes dohtor," after which the incident is given at some length.[4]

The exempla in the *Pastoral Care* are all taken from the Old Testament and consist largely of episodes from the lives of David, Nebuchadnezzar, Jeremiah, Isaiah, Hezekiah and Balaam. They are usually limited to four or five lines and are scattered promiscuously through the sections, sometimes occurring in groups of two or three. In many cases the exemplum is followed by a signification or "betokening" of its main features, with the aim of emphasizing its application to the point illustrated. Thus, after the tale of David soothing Saul by music, used to exemplify the effectiveness of dealing gently with the rich and proud, Saul's madness is said to signify the pride of the rich, and David, the humble life of holy men.[5] The fact that the narratives are all Biblical, and involve little or no originality on the part of the translator, renders further treatment unnecessary. They warrant attention simply as marking the first use of the type in our literature.

Alfred's translation of the *Consolation of Philosophy* is of greater importance for our study. Not only did this work have a more widespread influence,[6] but whereas the translator kept closely to the text of the *Cura Pastoralis*, he exercised

[2] *King Alfred's West Saxon Version of Gregory's Pastoral Care,* 196.

[3] *Ibid.,* 294.

[4] *Ibid.,* 415.

[5] *Ibid.,* 183–4.

[6] " Its influence and popularity, indeed, as a book of practical piety, can only be compared with the later *Imitation of Christ,* and the earlier Cicero's *De Officiis.* Hundreds of manuscripts are still to be found in dozens of libraries." W. J. Sedgefield, *King Alfred's Version of Boethius,* introd., xvi.

considerable freedom and originality in handling the text of
Boethius. Since the *Consolation* was written not merely for
the churchman, as was the *Pastoral Care,* but for the layman as
well, the presence of more popular illustrations is not surprising. There are fourteen exempla, all taken from history or
mythology, and ranging from a reference of two or three lines,
to complete stories, such that of Orpheus and Eurydice, or
Ulysses and Circe. Alfred utilized all but one of these,—that
narrating the heroic trials of Odysseus, Alcides, and others.
This exemplum, which occupies thirty-five lines in Boethius,[7]
is represented in Alfred's version by a general exhortation to
follow the examples of good and brave men.[8]

In spite of this obvious endorsement of exempla, Alfred
takes occasion to add to a mild apology for their appearance,
which he found in Boethius. Just before the tale of Orpheus
and Eurydice in the original, Philosophia says to Anima,
" Quod si rationes quoque non extra petitas sed intra rei quam
tractabamus ambitum collocatas agitavimus, nihil est quod
ammirere, cum Platone sanciente didiceris cognatos de quibus
loquuntur rebus oportere esse sermones."[9] Alfred translates
the passage as follows : " Þeah we nu scylen manega & mislica
bisna & bispell reccan, þeah hangaþ ure mod ealne weg on þæm
þe we æfterspyriaþ. Ne fo we no on þa bisna & on þa bispel
for þara leasena spella lufan, ac forþæmþe we woldon mid
gebecnan þa soþfæstnesse, & woldon þæt hit wurde to nytte
þam geherendum. Ic gemunde nu ryhte þæs wisan Platones
lara suma, hu he cwæþ þæt se mon se þe bispell secgan
wolde, ne sceolde fon on to ungelic bispell þære spræce þe he
þonne sprecan wolde."[10] Alfred's use in the foregoing passage
of the words " bisen " and " bispell " for Boethius' more general
term " rationes " is to be noted ; also the addition explaining
that he does not use exempla for the love of the stories but
because they help to make clear the truth.

Whether or not Alfred enjoyed the narratives, his belief in

[7] *Philosophiae Consolationis*, ed. Peiper, 118–19–20.
[8] *King Alfred's Old English Version of Boethius*, 139.
[9] *Philosophiae Consolationis*, ed. cit., 85.
[10] *King Alfred's Old English Version of Boethius*, 101.

their helpfulness is attested by his treatment of the original. Almost every narrative is expanded; in some cases, like that of Orpheus and Eurydice, doubled in length. He is always careful at the end of the exemplum to recall the moral which has been illustrated. In this also, he departs from his source at times. The tales are all told in a simple, naïve manner, with earnest desire to appeal to his readers. The following passages will serve to illustrate the charming simplicity of Alfred's narratives as well as other points of difference in treatment. In the Latin, Anima has asked Philosophia to clear up a certain point, at which Philosophia replies that as soon as one doubt is settled others spring up. She then proceeds to illustrate the difficulty: "Talis namque materia est, ut una dubitatione succisa innumerabiles aliae velut hydrae capita succrescant: nec ullus fuerit modus, nisi quis eas vivacissimo mentis igne coerceat."[11] The Old English version runs: "Swa swa mon on ealdspellum sægþ þæt an nædre wære þe hæfde nigon heafdu, & syle gif mon anra hwelc of aslog, þonne weoxon þær siofon on þæm anum heafde. Þa geberede hit þæt þær com se foremæra Erculus to, se wæs Iobes sunu; þa ne meahte he geþencan hu he hi mid ænige cræfte ofercuman sceolde, ær he hi bewæg mid wudu utan & forbærnde þa mid fyre. Swa is þisse spræce þe þu me æft acsast."[12] Alfred's narratives are not only longer than the originals, but, as this comparison indicates, more vivid and concrete. The later effect is obtained by the adding of specific names, definite numbers, explanatory clauses, the use of concrete terms, and the substitution of prose for poetry where such occurs in the Latin. This treatment of the narratives seems to show that Alfred not only believed in their efficacy, but that he had both studied and enjoyed them.

The purpose of the illustrations in the *Consolation* is two-fold: to make the points more clear and convincing, and to add to the interest of the treatise. The first of these, and probably the chief reason for inserting the exempla, is stated in the passage already quoted, where Alfred says that incidents are cited not for the love of stories but in order to aid in showing

[11] *Philosophiae Consolationis*, 108.
[12] *King Alfred's Old English Version of Boethius*, 127.

the truth with profit to the reader. The secondary purpose, the arousing of interest, undoubtedly seemed more important to Alfred than to Boethius. Therefore, in order to make the book more entertaining, he added to the exempla specific names, numbers, explanatory clauses, and in general vitalized them. In some cases the effectiveness of the original exemplum as an aid to clearness is somewhat lessened by the alterations, but Alfred's care in restating the point illustrated usually overcomes the defect. Irregularity in the handling of the type is, of course, frequent in both versions. In the Latin, the minor incidents are often mere references which appear without special distinction; a few more important ones, such as Orpheus and Eurydice, Circe's Cup, and The Hero's Path, are in verse at the close of sections. In the case of the translation, the illustrations are all in prose, and almost invariably run on without distinction. But notwithstanding the absence of conventional features, this work is a notable instance of the early use of exempla in English literature.[13]

Alfred's name is still further associated with exempla through the translation of the *Dialogues* of Gregory. It was due to him that Werferth, Bishop of Worcester,[14] undertook and completed the translation of this book into Old English. This early vernacular collection of exempla, with its original, constituted the chief influence on the use of the type during the Old English period.

Exempla in extant Old English literature are limited to Alfred's translations just examined, until the time of Werferth's translation of the *Dialogues.* From that time to the close of the twelfth century, they appear only in sermons. The representative collections which we shall examine are the *Blickling Homilies,* Aelfric's *Sermones,* the *Wulfstan Homilies, Old English Homilies of the Twelfth Century,* and the *Ormulum,* all of which follow closely the standard Latin models

[13] Alfred's figures of speech, which he loosely terms "examples," I shall not discuss. This subject has been treated by Dr. J. W. Tupper in his *Tropes and Figures in Anglo-Saxon Prose.*

[14] See H. Krebs, *Zur angelsächsischen Übersetzung der Dialoge Gregor's, Anglia,* II, 65–66.

of Gregory the Great, St. Augustine, and Beda. In the homilies of the last two, occurrence of exempla is negligible; only those of Gregory encouraged the use of the illustrative tale. On the other hand, symbolism[15] was employed by Beda, and especially by St. Augustine and Gregory, in the most thoroughgoing fashion. It is by far the most characteristic feature of the models upon which our English homilists based their discourses, and of the English homilies as well. From these facts, it is obvious why exempla are not particularly prominent in the homilies of the early period, and why external influence is largely attributable to Gregory the Great.

The *Blickling Homilies,* which we shall first consider, represent a period considerably earlier than the date of the manuscript (971) in which they are preserved. Both in vocabulary and syntactical structure, Aelfric's homilies (991–996) are distinctly more modern.[16] The *Blickling Homilies* are "not a homogeneous work, but a motley collection of sermons of various age and quality" which, generally speaking, "represents the preaching of the times before Aelfric."[17] For this reason a brief analysis of the structure of these homilies may be given to show the nature of Old English preaching. For convenience I shall divide the collection into two classes: the sermons for Sundays, and the sermons for Festival Days.

The general structural plan of the Sunday sermons consists of a Biblical passage followed by an exposition, usually symbolical. An outline of a typical sermon, the Homily for Shrove Sunday, will best serve to indicate the manner of development.

I A plain narrative of Jesus' ride to Jericho and the curing of the blind man.

II A statement that the narrative involves a mystery which must be explained in order to make clear its significance.

III The exposition according to the symbolical method.

[15] See above, p. 10, note.

[16] *Blickling Homilies,* preface, v–vi.

[17] See Earle, *Anglo-Saxon Literature,* 213–14; also *Cambridge History of English Literature,* I, 126 seq.

a The blind man signifies the blindness of all mankind after the Fall.

b The coming of Christ to Jericho signifies the
coming of Christ to light the path to eternal
life.

c The multitude which endeavored to restrain the
blind man signifies the carnal will and unrestrained lusts which exclude God's works.

d The blind man, asking for sight, not for silver or
gold, signifies that we should not seek for tran-
sitory things but for the light that never ends.

e The blind man sitting by the wayside represents
those who believe in God and follow Him.

IV Exhortations to forsake certain faults and to be mindful
of God's behests.[18]

Similarly, in the sermon for Palm Sunday, which is based
upon Jesus' ride upon the ass from Bethphage to Jerusalem,
Bethphage signifies the Holy Church; the two disciples symbolize holy teachers and the two loves necessary for eternal
life; the ass symbolizes the believing Jewish folk and others
subject to God's will; the crowd which went before Jesus
signifies the Jewish people, including the patriots and prophets.[19]
Each part of the signification gives rise to more or less conventional discussion on such topics as the present-day errors, ways
of betterment, the punishment of the wicked and the reward
of the righteous. The homilies are disjointed in style, as might
be expected from their early composition and eclectic borrowings from the Latin.

In the group just discussed, four exempla are used. Of
these, two are Biblical references: David's fight with Goliath,
and Judas burning in hell-fire for selling Christ.[20] A third is
related as an experience of St. Paul. Paul saw an old man led
by four " awyrgde englas," bound in chains, and cast into fiery
water up to his knees. Being questioned by Paul, the man con-
fessed that he was a bishop who had done more evil than

---

[18] *Blickling Homilies,* 14–24.

[19] *Ibid.,* 64–82.

[20] *Ibid.,* 30, 62 respectively.

good.[21] The narrative closes with a warning to present-day bishops that disobedience of God's law will be punished by the "fiery river" and the "iron hook." The fourth exemplum, illustrating the futility of riches and the disastrous results of an ungodly life, treats another important theme. After the death of a very rich man, his dearest friend left the country for sorrow. Upon returning, he visited the tomb of the departed. Here the dead man's bones spoke to him, reminding him that death was not far off, and exhorting him to turn from riches and pray to God. The man in sadness left the tomb and soon began to study and teach God's law, whereby he earned divine grace and saved other souls from torment.[22] The homilist then remarks, "Magon we þonne, men þa leofestan, us þis to gemyndum habban & þas bysene on urum heortum staþelian, þæt we ne sceolan lufian worlde glengas to swiþe ne þysne middangeard." These last two exempla deal with themes greatly favored by later preachers and collectors: i. e., wicked and avaricious churchmen horribly punished by fiends; and warnings of the deceased to the living.[23]

The festival sermons of the *Blickling Homilies* make no use of tales to point moral or religious doctrine. At the same time this group consists almost wholly of narratives dealing with the lives of the Virgin and the apostles. The incidents, often of an extremely lurid tone and in many cases lacking Biblical authority, are given as facts with absolute assurance and no qualification.[24] In the sermon on the Assumption of Mary, for

[21] *Blickling Homilies,* 42. This exemplum is taken from apochryphal writings. Earle points out (*op. cit.,* 215) that certain books, such as furnished material for the *B. H.* were, in the eighth or ninth century, put on the index. Some of these were: the *Acts of Pilate, Journeys of the Apostles, Acts of Peter, Acts of Andrew the Apostle,* the *Contradiction of Solomon,* the *Physiologus.* See "Prohibited Books" in the *Dictionary of Christian Antiquities.*

[22] *Ibid.,* 112.

[23] On the latter class, see M. B. Heaureau, *Les Récits d'Apparitions dans les Sermons du Moyen Age,* in *Mémoires de l'Academie des Inscriptions et Belles-Lettres,* XXVIII, Pt. II, 239 seq.

[24] The marked contrast between these sermons and those of Aelfric is noteworthy. It is quite likely that Aelfric had the *Blickling Homilies* in mind when he wrote in the preface to his *Sermones Catholici,* "Then

example, a vivid and detailed account of her translation into heaven is given.[25] In the sermon on Peter and Paul appears a long narrative of a wonderful contest between Peter and the sorcerer Simon, which for startling features rivals a similar strife between Friar Bacon and Friar Bungay.[26] The Dedication of St. Michael's Church contains, among other marvelous things, an account of how one Garganus tried to shoot an unruly bull, but was himself killed by the arrow which the wind turned back; also of the marvelous footprints before the church door.[27] The Festival of St. Martin recounts wonderful resuscitations by that saint.[28] The festival of St. Andrew contains a number of such absurd narratives as the appearance of the cross on St. Andrew's face, his flesh and hair turning into a fruit-bearing tree, a stone image sending out a stream of brine from its mouth at his bidding.[29] These instances are representative of a large number which form the body of the festival-day discourses.

Tht *Blickling Homilies,* as has been shown, employ few narratives as illustrations. Two of the four noted are, indeed, of particular importance, since they represent two favorite exemplum themes: wicked men punished by fiends; and warnings from the dead.[30] The festival group with its fantastic incidents indicates the vogue of narrative sermons based on the lives of holy men; it also shows lack of restraint on the part of the preachers, and the marvelous credulity of contemporary audiences.

it occurred to my mind . . . that I would turn this book from the Latin language into the English tongue; not from confidence of great learning, but because I have seen and heard of much error in many English books, which unlearned men through their simplicity have esteemed as great wisdom." *Homilies of the Anglo-Saxon Church,* I, 3.

[25] Aelfric frankly admits that he is not prepared to state, as some have done, that Mary was translated. See *Homilies,* II, 444.

[26] *Blickling Homilies,* 172 seq.

[27] *Ibid.,* 198–204.

[28] *Ibid.,* 216–18.

[29] *Ibid.,* 242–44.

[30] Aelfric states that "we read everywhere in books" that men have died and afterward returned to tell their experiences. *Homilies,* II, 355.

The generally low state of learning and morality in the
Church of the period which produced the *Blickling Homilies*
was gradually changing for the better as Aelfric's time approached. His homilies, written between 991 and 996, show in
their sanity and literary excellence, the effects of the reformation which originated in France and was carried on in England
by Dunstan, Aethelwold and Odo.[31]

Aelfric's homilies were probably compiled from the sources
which he mentions in his preface: Augustine, Jerome, Beda,
Gregory, Smaragdus, and Haymo.[32] In this preface, Aelfric
states that he translates these sermons from Latin books into
"simple English" so that the hearts of those readers or
listeners who know only their native tongue, can be reached.
He adds that he does not translate word for word, but sense
for sense. The editor, Thorpe, states in his preface that he
is not able to say whether Aelfric was a mere translator or
whether he drew from his own stores. He gives his opinion,
however, that no one of his homilies is, generally speaking, a
translation from any one Latin original, but rather a compilation from several.[33] This, it seems to me, is pretty clearly
indicated by such statements as that in which Aelfric says that
he will expound the gospel according to the authority of Augustine and Gregory.[34] Moreover, his efforts to adapt his

[31] On Dunstan and his times, see *Memorials of Saint Dunstan, Archbishop of Canterbury,* introd. See also Earle, *Anglo-Saxon Literature,* 219.
[32] *Homilies,* I, 1.
[33] *Ibid.,* editor's preface, vi. Max Förster's conclusions on this point
are as follows: "Von einer wort-für-wort-übersetzung, wie solche z. b. in
den *Blickling Homilies* vorkommen, kann nirgends bei Aelfric die rede
sein; . . . es handelt sich dort fast immer um erklärungen zum Bibeltexte,
die in ganz freier weise mit beibehaltung der schlagwörter wiedergegeben
sind. Ein weiteres moment für die relative selbstständigkeit der homilien
ergiebt sich daraus, dass wohl die hälfte nicht auf einer vorlage beruht,
sondern aus mehreren zusammengearbeitet ist. Das verhältnis der quellen
zu einander kann sich hierbei recht mannigfaltig gestalten; meist beschränkt
sich der beitrag der zweiten oder dritten quelle auf wenige sätze, oft
anknüpfend an eingeschobene citate; doch kommt auch nicht selten vor,
dass zwei quellen sich gegenseitig die wage halten." *Über die Quellen von
Aelfric's Homiliae Catholicae,* 9–10. For a good study of Aelfric's life and
writings, see Miss C. L. White's *Aelfric.*
[34] *Homilies,* II, 227; see also 536.

discourses to his audiences point to considerable originality of treatment. Probably the main doctrinal features, such as the interpretations of Scriptural passages and statements of dogmatic points, are freely translated from the Latin sources which best treated the particular matters under discussion; the arrangement of material, the allotment of proportion, and the selection of illustrations, may be attributed mainly to Aelfric.

A rapid glance at the homilies will indicate why adaptation was necessary and will suggest how the preacher was continually regulating his discourses by the character of his audiences. In the first place, as the preface and the prayer at the end of the collection show, the homilies were written chiefly for the unlearned. The scholarship of Gregory, Jerome, and St. Augustine, although it might serve as a basis, needed simplification. Then too, Aelfric sometimes addresses special classes, a group of girls (mædenlica heap),[35] a monastic body (munuchades mannum),[36] or maidens and pure widows.[37] The main reason for special treatment of his subject was his keen realization of the inability of the audience to understand the depth of the gospel as expounded by his great predecessors. "We might," he says in a thoroughly characteristic passage, "more elaborately expound this holy text, according to the interpretation of Augustine, but we doubt whether ye can accurately judge of the greater deepness therein."[38] Time and again he states that the gospel has a hidden meaning which is entirely beyond the comprehension of his hearers.[39] In consequence of this he takes great pains to present the symbolical significance of the text in a simple manner. At the same time, he writes with recognition of his hearers' limit of endurance. He says, for example, "One should speak to laymen according to the measure of their understanding, so that they be not disheartened by the deepness, nor by the length wearied."[40] In other places he asks patience while he proceeds.

[35] *Homilies*, I, 437.
[36] *Ibid.*, I, 401.
[37] *Ibid.*, I, 447.
[38] *Ibid.*, I, 557.
[39] *Ibid.*, I, 167, 581 ; II, 189, 447.
[40] *Ibid.*, II, 447.

Occasionally he avowedly foregoes a part of the exposition
and closes his sermon with such a statement as the following:
"Tedious it would be for us to recount and for you to hear all
the depths of the great Baptist's preaching;"[41] or, in another
place, "This exposition is longsome for you to hear, but we
will now here end our speech."[42] The foregoing facts suggest
not only a considerable amount of originality in the composition of the homilies, but a comprehension of his audience far
beyond that of his English predecessors.

Possessing this comprehension, Aelfric tried to make his
homilies clear and attractive. As a means to this end he recognized the exemplum and spoke clearly in favor of it. In one
of his sermons he says: "This epistle is very complex for us
to expound and very deep for you to hear. It does not now
seem good to us to speak more concerning it, but we will relate
for your bettering some other edifying matter of the great
mother of God."[43] He then tells two legends showing how
the intervention of the Virgin saved those who worshipped her.
Again, in praising the preaching of St. Cuthbert, Aelfric states
that "a his bodunga mid gebysnungum astealde, and eac mid
wundrum wel geglengde."[44] In another place he suggests to
his audience the reading of Gregory's *Dialogues,* which, he
says, have been turned into English.[45] But, as has been stated,
Aelfric was a product of the reform movement, a scholar and
an earnest teacher. He himself was not carried away by the
wild narratives in the *Blickling Homilies,* nor did he intend that
his audiences should be misled by accounts from questionable
sources.

In view of the effect which this conservatism had upon
Aelfric's use of exempla, it may be well to examine briefly
his view of the preacher's duty. That it was, like Gregory's,
an exalted one, may be seen in the noble expressions running
through the homily on the Nativity of Several Apostles. Here
he maintains that the teaching of Christ's lore is the business of

[41] *Homilies,* I, 363 ; see also I, 449, 557 ; II, 467.
[42] *Ibid.,* II, 537.
[43] *Ibid.,* I, 449.
[44] *Ibid.,* II, 148.
[45] *Ibid.,* II, 359.

the preacher; that the world is full of priests, but that few are working in God's vineyard; that ministers should work not merely for temporal reward; that they should salt the minds of men with wisdom.[46] It is in the spirit of this last sentiment particularly, that he guards against the extravagance of apochryphal and exaggerated legendary accounts. "If we should say more," Aelfric observes in one of the homilies, "of this feast-day than we read in the holy books that have been composed by the inspiration of God, then we should be like unto those heretics, who from their own imagination, or from dreams, have recorded many false traditions; but the orthodox teachers, Augustine, Jerome, Gregory, and many others, have, through their wisdom, rejected them. These heretical works, nevertheless, yet exist, both in Latin and in English, and ignorant men read them. It is enough for believing men to read and to say that which is true."[47] Frequently he warns his audience against going beyond the evidence of the gospel in such matters as the Assumption, Jesus raising the dead, and the vision of St. Paul.[48] This does not mean that Aelfric was altogether averse to using legendary material, as its presence in the homilies, as well as his later compilation of saints' lives, testifies. But even in the preface to the *Saints' Lives,* he again voices the conservative attitude. "I do not promise, however, to write very many in this tongue because it is not fitting that many should be translated into our language, lest peradventure the pearls of Christ be had in disrespect. And therefore I hold my peace as to the book called *Vitae Patrum,* wherein are contained many subtle points which ought not to be laid open to the laity, nor are we ourselves quite able to fathom them."[49] Having in mind Aelfric's free use of his sources, his appreciation of the needs of his audience, and his spirit of conservatism, we may proceed to examine his use of the exemplum.

Although there are certain differences, Aelfric's use closely resembles that of thirteenth and fourteenth century writers.

[46] *Homilies,* II, 529–537.
[47] *Ibid.,* II, 445.
[48] *Ibid.,* I, 441, II, 445; I, 495; II, 333, respectively.
[49] *Lives of Saints,* 3.

The characteristic features of illustrative narratives at the height of their vogue were as follows: (1) the tales were ordinarily striking, often lurid or indelicate; (2) they were rarely taken from the Bible, but represented a vast range of sources, religious and secular; (3) tales about churchmen outnumbered all other kinds; (4) they were not mere references, but incidents with a beginning, middle and end; (5) exempla were not excluded from the body of the sermon or treatise, but the favorite place was at the close, where from one to five usually appeared; (6) conventional introductory and closing phrases very often set off the exemplum; (7) in a great many instances the source of the narrative was given; e. g., "We read in the Dialogues," or " Cesarius tells of a hermit." Such are the characteristics of the tales in the *North-English Homily Collection* or Mirk's *Festial*. In the homilies of Aelfric may be found cases which illustrate practically all of these features.

Taking up the exempla with reference to the points just noted, we shall first consider the character of the tales. From what has been said regarding Aelfric's conservatism, it may be expected that they will not be lurid and exaggerated. A number of the tales are, of course, better adapted to a more credulous age than our own in that they involve the supernatural; such, for instance, is the tale from the *Dialogues* telling of a Valerian noble who was carried off by black fiends because of his sinful life; or the tale from Beda, about Ymma's fetters being loosened by his brother's singing masses.[50] Two of the exempla are of the lurid type. One of these from the *Vitae Patrum* relates how in answer to prayer for a proof of transubstantiation, an angel appeared and with a knife carved up a child in the sacred dish. When the monks went to examine it, the body and blood was changed to bread and wine.[51] The second instance of this kind, which Aelfric takes from Gregory, tells of a bad monk who on his death-bed was about to be swallowed by a dragon, when the prayers of good

[50] *Homilies*, I, 413; II, 357, respectively.

[51] *Ibid.*, II, 273. It is to be remembered that Aelfric looked somewhat askance at the *Vitae Patrum*.

[52] *Ibid.*, I, 533.

4

monks drove away the monster.[52]   But the great majority of exempla in these homilies are moderate in character and are related with little attempt to lay stress upon startling or dramatic features.   This generally conservative tone is in part explained by the kind of sources from which he drew his illustrations.

They are taken mainly from the *Bible* and Gregory's *Dialogues;* in addition to these sources, legends of the Virgin, Beda's *Ecclesiastical History,* and the *Vitae Patrum* are sparingly used.   The Biblical narratives are the following: Gehazi stricken with leprosy for taking a bribe, Hezekiah's victory over Sennacherib, three youths in the fiery oven, Daniel in the lion's den, the apostles freed from prison by an angel, the child cured by its mother's faith, the rich man called to account, Jesus stilling the tempest, Jesus casting out devils, the parable of the unfruitful tree, Nebuchadnezzar turned into a beast, Belshazzar's feast.[53]   Besides these twelve developed narratives, there are a number of Biblical references used as exempla.[54]   These are often grouped, as are the longer ones, to get a cumulative effect.

The source of next importance is Gregory, from whom Aelfric takes nine exempla, exclusive of the incidents in the festival sermons.   They are: Martyrius and the leper (Christ), the Valerian noble seized by fiends, the bad monk saved from the dragon, the joyful death of the holy Servulus, transubstantiation proved by the bloody finger, the blasphemous child carried off by the devil, the report of a man returned from death, the glorious end of patient Stephen, Romula blessed for resignation to palsy.[55]

There remain seven exempla, which were taken from three well-known sources.   Beda's *History* furnished the tale of Ymma and Tunna; the *Vitae Patrum* is the source of the child carved at the altar, the man who entertained a stranger (Christ), the death of the heretic Arius, the death of the

[53] *Homilies,* I, 401, 569, 571, 571, 573; II, 51, 105, 379, 379, 407, 433, 435, resp.

[54] *Ibid.,* I, 483, 489, 525, 575; II, 79, 107, 326, 331.

[55] *Ibid.,* I, 337, 413, 533; II, 97, 273, 327, 355, 547, 547, resp.

heretic Sabellius. A collection of Mary legends furnished Theophilus saved from the devil, and Basilius' victory over Julian.[56] In all, then, aside from the dozen or so brief references, the *Homilies* contain twenty-eight exempla, taken from five sources: the *Bible,* Gregory's *Dialogues,* the *Vitae Patrum,* legends of the Virgin, and Beda's *Ecclesiastical History.* Of these, the *Bible* and the *Dialogues* are by far the most important contributors. The subdued tone of the stories taken from Gregory, and the large number of Biblical tales, give a moderation which contrasts with the later use of exempla, when the lurid story was not avoided and the *Bible* was but rarely cited.

We have now to consider the literary handling of the tales. In the works previously examined, the exempla have been, in the main, brief and almost altogether lacking in artistic construction. Aelfric's narratives make a considerable advance beyond the brief Biblical references of the *Pastoral Care,* and the short, rather brusque narratives of Alfred's *Boethius* and the *Blickling Homilies.* A few of Aelfric's tales, such as the death of the heretic Sabellius (six lines), and the man who returned from death (half page), are brief. But the great majority occupy from three quarters of a page to two pages in the text. They have, moreover, the form of completely rounded incidents with a beginning, middle and end. The Biblical passages are related with considerable detail and in a familiar style. These, together with the translations from Gregory, make the narratives a very admirable body of exempla. The type in Aelfric's homilies becomes unquestionably a literary form of no little importance.

An advance toward the conventional in the position and number of exempla, and introductory and closing phrases, is also to be noted. There is a marked tendency to place the exempla at the end of the homilies, as we might expect from Aelfric's understanding of the mental state of his

[56] *Homilies,* II, 357, 273, 287; I, 291, 291, 449, 445, resp. The last two *contes dévots* represent a class which was much favored by those who collected or used exempla. The legends cited may be found in *Les Miracles de la Sainte Vierge traduits et mis en vers par Gautier de Coincy,* 26 seq., and 395 seq., resp.

audiences. In six cases we find tales in medial positions; three times they are placed near the end; and in twelve instances they appear at the close of the discourse. As a rule, a given homily has but one or two narratives or references, but in a few cases more are cited. In one instance we find three developed incidents and three outlines, which were very likely expanded in the spoken discourse.[57] This grouping for cumulative effect is most noticeable in the case of Biblical references.[58] Also in opening and closing the exempla, Aelfric's manner resembles that of the flourishing period. For purposes of comparison I shall cite a typical instance from the *Festial* of Mirk. After speaking of God's grace, the writer warns his readers not to abide in their sins, for God's patience is not everlasting. He then says: "For þagh he abyde long, at þe last he woll smyte suche þat woll not amende hom; and when he smytyth, he smytyth sore.

NARRACIO

I rede þat þer was a knyght," etc., to the effect that the knight sinned and was warned by a voice from heaven that at the end of thirty years he should feel vengeance. At the expiration of the period he and all his companious sunk with his strong castle into the earth. Then follows a new section, beginning:

"þus ye may se, þagh God abyde longe, at þe last he smytyth sore. Wherfor I amonysh you, þat ye take not hys grace of abydyng yn vayne."[59] In some cases the section preceding the narrative ended with such a phrase as "Herby I may schewe you an ensampull," or "But forto undyrstond þys þe bettyr, I schew þys ensampull," or "And yet, forto styr you more in concyens, y tell you þys ensampull." Again, the tale did not always close a section but was sometimes followed by a brief moralization or restatement of the point illustrated by the tale. The conventional opening "I rede," which is very frequent with Mirk, is sometimes varied by such ex-

[57] *Homilies,* I, 569–575.

[58] *Ibid.,* I, 525–27, 483, 489, 569–75; II, 379, 433–37. Many of the festival homilies, as in the case of the *Blicklings,* contain much narrative matter but no incidents for illustrative purposes.

[59] *Festial,* Pt. I, 88–89.

pressions as, " Seynt Gregory tellyþ," " An ensampull of þys I fynd, as Alisander Nekkam tellyþ "; or, at times the tale opens without such phrases, as, " In þe towne of Schrosbury sytten þre men togedyr."

A comparison of Aelfric's handling of exempla with Mirk's as indicated above, gives further evidence that a formal use of the type existed thus early in English literature. Most of Aelfric's exempla either occupy the entire section, or at least open the section, which is closed by a return to the point illustrated. Again, as in the *Festial,* the tales are frequently introduced by such formal phrases as, " We have a very manifest example of this thing," " Gregory has related an example," or, " We read in the book that is called ' Vitae Patrum.' " The moralizations following the exempla are also similar to the typical forms of the fourteenth century. For instance, after narrating the horrible death of Arius, Aelfric says, " Thus God manifested that he was as void in his inside as he had before been in his belief."[60] Similarly, after the story of Gehazi, a new section begins, " Now it is therefore for monastic men to shun with great care these evil examples."[61] At other times he uses such expressions as, " From this it is manifest." Of course, the conventionality which results from using the same expression in scores of instances, as is the case in a work like the *Festial* or the *Book of the Knight of La Tour Landry,* is not to be found in Aelfric's score and a half of exempla. The point to be noted is the essential resemblance between Aelfric and the writers of the thirteenth and fourteenth centuries in the handling of the type.

In the foregoing sections it has been shown that Aelfric's conservatism largely excluded from his homilies the unrestrained narratives used by an earlier school of English preachers; that, understanding his audiences, he saw the need and efficacy of exempla, as had his most quoted model, Gregory; that in the number and kind of exempla used, and in the manner of handling them, Aelfric not only advances beyond his English predecessors, but resembles the preachers of the thirteenth and fourteenth centuries.

[60] *Homilies,* I, 291.
[61] *Ibid.,* I, 401.

Next to be considered is the collection of fifty-four homilies[62] attributed by Wanley to Wulfstan, Archbishop of York from 1002 to 1023. As the canon stands at present, seven are accepted as unquestionably written by Wulfstan, and eight others as probably from his pen.[63] These fifteen homilies have been removed from the whole group with considerable effort. "The difficulties," says Dr. Kinard, "attending any attempt to separate the genuine homilies in this collection from the spurious are emphasized by all critics who have expressed themselves on the subject."[64] From this it appears probable that the Wanley collection, taken as a whole, represents the school of Wulfstan. For the purposes of this study, discrimination in the matter of authorship would be of no particular value; I shall, therefore, refer to the whole group as the Wulfstan homilies.

Before discussing these homilies it is desirable to recall the condition of the times which produced them. The comparatively peaceful period during which the scholarly Aelfric composed his homilies changed rapidly into the stormy period in which Wulfstan wrote.[65] Trouble with the Danes and Northmen had been growing through Aethelred's reign (978–1016), and finally in 1002 the king, in order to win the friendship of Normandy, married Emma, the Norman Duke's daughter. The same dread of invasion led to the massacre of the Northern mercenaries on St. Brice's Day, 1002, by the king's order. "Wedding and murder, however," says Green, "proved feeble defences against Swegen. His fleet reached the coast in 1003,

---

[62] *Wulfstan; Sammlung der ihm zugeschriebenen Homilien nebst Untersuchungen über ihre Echtheit*, published by A. S. Napier. In the year preceding his publication of this edition, Napier brought out a study of Wulfstan's work, *Uber die Werke des altenglischen Erzbishofs Wulfstan*, in which he concluded that the attribution of Wanley was in great part erroneous. To those admitted by Napier, Dr. J. P. Kinard has added a few others. See *A Study of Wulfstan's Homilies*, 32 seq.

[63] Unquestioned, Nos. 2, 3, 19, 22, 23, 33, 34; probable, Nos. 5, 10, 12, 13, 14, 15, 17, 27. (Napier's numbering.)

[64] Kinard, *op. cit.*, 11.

[65] The raiding expeditions which occurred before 1002 were not to be compared with the destructive ravages after that date. See E. A. Freeman, *The History of the Norman Conquest of England*, I, 285 seq.

and for four years he marched through the length and breadth of southern and eastern England 'lighting his war beacons as he went' in blazing homestead and town. Then for a heavy bribe he withdrew, to prepare for a later and more terrible onset. But there was no rest for the realm. The fiercest of the Norwegian jarls took his place, and from Wessex the war extended over Mercia and East Anglia. In 1012 Canterbury was taken and sacked, Aelfheah the Archbishop dragged to Greenwich, and there in default of ransom brutally slain. . . . Meanwhile the court was torn with intrigue and strife. . . . Eadric, whom Aethelred raised to be Ealdorman of Mercia, became a power that overawed the crown. In this paralysis of the central authority all organization was lost. 'Shire would not help other' when Swegen returned in 1013. The war was terrible but short. Everywhere the country was pitilessly harried, churches plundered, men slaughtered."[66] Swegen died in 1014, but under Cnut the contest was maintained until the latter was made king and peace was established. In all this time the Church was the center of national resistance.[67]

Produced in such a time by intense men, the Wulfstan homilies are concerned less with long expositions of Scripture than with vital issues of the day. Likewise the scholarly and literary style of Aelfric's homilies changes to a more practical and vigorous tone in the Wulfstan group. Poetic and figurative words give way to familiar, concrete words; the use of tropes, similes, and symbolism becomes rare. With the feeling of those who realize deeply and would better the evil conditions of men and the times, the writers constantly strive for clearness and directness even at the cost of felicity of expression and literary interest.

A corresponding change in exempla takes place. The employment of non-Biblical tales, which was so frequent in Ael-

[66] J. R. Green, *History of the English People,* I, 98–99; see also Freeman, *op. cit.,* I, 285 seq.

[67] Green, *op. cit.,* I, 100. In spite of this, it is to be remembered that the Church from the early years of Aethelred's reign was on the decline. With the accession of Cnut came a short period of improvement; still "religion declined . . . and a general inefficiency and indifference prevailed in the Church as in the State." H. D. Traill, *Social England,* I, 163.

fric's homilies, decreases and Biblical narratives are again largely depended upon to illustrate and confirm doctrine. Most of the citations are from the Old Testament. The following undeveloped themes appear as illustrations: Adam's loss of Paradise, the burning of Job's possessions, Adam admonished by the angels, David's conversion, the conversion of the Ninivites.[68] These five references of which two are repeated, are given briefly, with little or no detail. The same number of developed Biblical tales, two of which are repeated, are used as exempla: how Jonathas lost a battle by breaking a fast, Noah's flood, the destruction of Dathon, Abiron, and Choreb, the death of the Sunday laborer, the rich man called to account.[69] To these may be added two apocryphal tales: Peter's victory over Simon the sorcerer, and St. Paul's account of a contest over an expiring soul.[70] There are in all, then, sixteen Biblical exempla. This is, as a comparison of the non-Biblical narratives will show, a very large percentage of the entire number. It is to be noted that four incidents are repeated, and that nearly all of the illustrations exemplify the results of wrong-doing.

How may this marked preference for Biblical illustrations be explained? It is not likely that it was due to ignorance of other material. Wulfstan and his school were undoubtedly more or less familiar with Beda's *History,* the *Consolation of Philosophy,* Gregory's *Dialogues,* the *Vitae Patrum,* saints' lives, and probably with Aldhelm's *De Laudibus Virginitatis,* which contained a large number of non-Biblical exempla. Aelfric's homilies, moreover, furnished an immediate precedent for the use of such illustrations. In my opinion the explanation lies rather in the practical adaptation of illustration to text. The insistent thought running through the Wulfstan homilies centers around the sins and short-comings of men, and the terrible punishments which await those who will not reform. The best, most convenient and authoritative illustrations of that theme were Biblical. For instance, the preacher urges

[68] *Wulfstan Homilies,* 69, 97, 103, 170 (repeated, 172), 170 (repeated, 173), resp.

[69] *Ibid.,* 174, 206 (repeated, 216), 219 (repeated, 295), 220, 257, resp.

[70] *Ibid.,* 98, 234, resp.

the avoidance of breaking fast; as an illustration of the dire
results which attend a violation of the ordinance, the case
of Jonathas and the lost battle is both apt and convincing.
Or, the preacher attacks Sabbath-breaking, and the fate of
Dathon and his companions comes to mind without necessitat-
ing search. To men like Aelfric, of greater literary inclina-
tion and more given to theological exposition of the Scriptures,
the symbolism of the Church Fathers, the legends, and the
Dialogues of Gregory, made a greater appeal. To men of
intense reforming zeal like Wulfstan and his followers, the
Bible was first and foremost.

The non-Biblical exempla, though fewer, are of importance
because of their character. They are four in number: a young
monk who sang from heaven to his mother, the sinner's soul
which dared not leave the body, a devil's account of hell, an
account of hell by a Scot returned from death.[71] The tale of
the young monk is a detached exemplum standing alone as
number XXXI of Napier's edition.[72] That it was used as an
exemplum in some homily is clear from the opening, "We
willaþ nu secgan sume bysne to þisum." The story tells of a
boy who was wont to sing among the monks. His mother
came often to hear him, but was one day disappointed; the boy
had disappeared. Finally, at the mother's entreaty, the abbot
prayed that the boy might be allowed to sing from heaven. In
response to the prayer, his voice rang out loud and clear,
showing that he was with God whom he had served. This
tale is unusually delightful both in subject-matter and quiet
manner of telling. It seems distinctly out of place among this
set of homilies.

The other three narratives are of an entirely different character. The first of these deals with a soul which dared not
leave the body for fear of the "awyrgedan gastas" which
stood before it. The soul upbraids the body, while a devil

---

[71] *Homilies,* 152, 140, 146 (repeated in variant form, 214), 205 (repeated
in part, twice in the same homily, and twice in the following homily),
resp.

[72] The editor's note on this tale (p. 152) runs: "Nur in E [Bodleian,
Junius 99] enthalten. Keine überschrift; die seitenüberschrift, die nicht
vom schreiber herrührt, lautet XVI Be ane munuccilde."

cries out to his associates, "stingaþ stranglic sar" on his eyes, mouth and heart; after this, the unfortunate victim is further tortured by a sight of the joy of heaven, and is then hurled into the mouth of a fiery dragon which spews him into the hottest fires of hell-punishment.

The story of Nial, the Scottish deacon, is broken up and told in parts through two sermons. It narrates how this man was dead five weeks and then returned to tell of the awful fire that awaited those who disobeyed God's law against Sabbath-breaking.

The tale of the devil and the hermit relates how the devil told the hermit that the earth compared in size to hell was as a pin prick to a broad surface (bradum brede). He also told the hermit that if hell were fenced in with iron and filled with fire, and surrounded with bellows, each blown by a man with the strength of Samson; and if an iron roof were put over this fire and covered with men, and each of these men had a hammer in his hands; and though the men blew all the bellows and the others beat the hammers on the iron roof,—if this should be done, there would not be experienced what a single night in hell brought forth. The second version of this tale in the homilies is different. Here, in reply to the hermit's question as to the nature of hell, the devil says that though seven men should sit on the earth and they could speak in every tongue, "þara is twa and hundseofontig," and each man were to live forever, and each of them had seven heads, and each head had seven tongues, and each tongue had an iron voice, they could not tell of all the punishment of hell.

Two of the tales discussed represent favorite stock exempla: the soul of a dying person attacked by devils, and a person returned from death to tell of the other world.[73] The last tale, dealing with the devil and the hermit, was to be found, according to the homilist, "on halgum bocum," so the idea was apparently common also. Of course there are in later sermons and collections, stories in which devils have dealings with hermits, but the naïvely terrific form of these exempla in the Wulfstan

[73] Both of these stories have analogues in Beda; see *Ecclesiastical History*, I, 285, 294.

homilies is almost unique. The aim of this narrative is the same as that of the two preceding. Indeed, the whole body of exempla in these homilies is homogeneous in that they serve practically one purpose,—to frighten the audience by the consequences of wrong-doing. To this end no pains seem to have been spared to make the people tremble, since even the Biblical incidents are often recounted in a manner which makes the original seem mild.[74]

As a formal type, the exemplum is not as marked in the Wulfstan group as in the homilies of Aelfric. The Biblical incidents are short, and, though forcible, are crudely, baldly told. The non-Biblical narratives are longer and more complete, but they lack the rounded development of the legends related by Aelfric. Besides this lack of literary quality, there are other departures from form. The exempla are rarely reserved till the end of the homilies, but occur wherever occasion requires; nor are they introduced with formal expressions. In a couple of instances we find, "betere eac, þæt we nu sum to bysne secgan," and, "uton niman us nu ealle bysne be Saule þam cinicge,"[75] opening the illustration. But these are exceptions to the usual abrupt transition from the abstract observation to the tale. Such fixed phrases as, "we read," or "I find," are also wanting. On the other hand, the exempla are usually followed by a varying form of request that the auditors or readers benefit by the tale just related. Such expressions as, "Let us, therefore, turn to the Lord and forsake evil"; "That may serve as an example for us"; or, "Lo, we may perceive by this," are not uncommon. These are, however, an entirely natural accompaniment of narratives with a purpose.

The present examination of the Wulfstan group has shown that the homilies are largely concerned with making the Scrip-

[74] There can be little doubt that exaggeration was not a willful imposture on the part of the clergy at this time. Probably they believed to a considerable extent the wondrous things they narrated. The Venerable Beda himself recounts in his *History* the experience of one who returned from the dead. This account vies in terror not only with the exempla in Wulfstan, but with the pictures in Dante's *Inferno,* to which it has a curious resemblance; see *Eccl. Hist.,* I, 287 seq.

[75] *Homilies,* 98, 174, resp.

tures bear directly upon everyday life, and that the style is adapted to this end. The exempla, both in the kind selected and in the manner of treatment, express the simplicity and unrestrained ardor of popular reformers. Brief and familiar Biblical incidents, crudely but forcibly stated, point out the fearful fate of the evil-doer.[76] A small number of non-Biblical exempla of a kind which persisted throughout the history of the type, answers the same purpose. A tone of exaggeration, unqualified by literary niceties, pervades them all. The unfixed position of the exempla, and the virtual absence of conventional features, give further indication that Wulfstan and his followers used the type with serious motives, never merely to follow custom, to consume time, or to satisfy the popular taste.

From the Wulfstan homilies we pass to the collection, largely of the twelfth century, known as the *Old English Homilies.* In the opinion of Morris, those of the First Series possess comparatively little originality, but are made up from Aelfric and "compilations from older documents of the eleventh century."[77] Three of the *Old English Homilies,* numbers IX, X, and XXIV, are, as he points out, taken substantially from three of Aelfric's. In one of the other homilies, number XI, is inserted a passage drawn from another of Aelfric's.[78] The original texts of the remaining homilies have not been found, but Morris believes that they also are copied from older documents of the eleventh century. With reference to the Second Series, he concludes, though he has not found evidences of transcription, that since five homilies of this series are found also in the manuscript of the First Series, "these, if not many other homilies of this [Second] series, are transcripts."[79] He further states that most of them were, perhaps, translated from

[76] It is noteworthy that Sabbath-breaking is more constantly and harshly dealt with than any other evil treated in this collection.

[77] *Old English Homilies,* edited by Richard Morris, *First Series,* preface, xi.

[78] The original of No. IX is found in Thorpe's *Aelfric,* I, 311. The original of No. X is found in *O. E. H., First Series,* Appendix II. The original of No. XXIV is found in Thorpe's *Aelfric,* I, 9. The original of the passage in No. XI is found in Thorpe's *Aelfric,* I, 217.

[79] See *O. E. H., Second Series,* preface, vii.

Latin homilies, though some of them have the appearance of original compositions.[80] The above statements lead to the conclusion that the *Old English Homilies,* where not original, were transcribed from earlier English homilies, which, in turn, were based upon still earlier Latin homilies.

Vollhardt takes a different position with reference to some of the homilies, and with a fair degree of plausibility advocates a direct late-Latin source. His summary is as follows: "Several, at least, of our homilies, may be explained by the acceptation of some late-Latin model, written in the twelfth century; a model in which Augustinian and Gregorian passages are already changed and worked over as we have seen in the citations of the English homilies before us; a model in which, moreover, literal borrowings from Ambrosius, Paulus Diaconus, Ovid, Horace, have found favor. All these requirements can, in my opinion, be furnished only by the work of a French or Norman clergyman, not that of an Anglo-Saxon, as the citations from Bernard of Clairvaux, etc., have shown to be impossible."[81] Vollhardt's citations of parallel passages from the Latin homilies of Bernard of Clairvaux and Radulfus Ardens, who flourished about 1100, make it seem extremely probable that such sources were used. The probability is increased when we consider the power which had been wielded by French clerics in England since the middle of the eleventh century.[82]

What conclusions, then, may be reached as to the composition of the *Old English Homilies?* In my opinion there seems to have been, generally speaking, too much insistence upon wholesale copying from single sources, and not enough allowance made for originality and eclectic borrowing on the part of the homilists. The substantial agreement between numbers IX, X, and XXIV of the present collection and three of Aelfric's, warrants a practically unqualified conclusion. But when, for

---

[80] *O. E. H. Sec. Ser.,* preface, ix.

[81] W. Vollhardt, *Der Einfluss der lateinischen geistlichen Litteratur auf einige kleinere Schöpfungen der englischen Übergangsperiode,* 17.

[82] "A man might now [in 1051] go from the Straits of Dover to the Humber, over Kentish, East-Saxon, and Danish ground, without once in the course of his journey going out of the spiritual jurisdiction of Norman prelates." Freeman, *History of the Norman Conquest,* II, 159.

example, one homily in the collection has a passage certainly borrowed from Aelfric;[83] another homily has a passage almost certainly taken from Gregory, and a quotation from St. Ambrose;[84] another has a passage which is obviously original;[85] and still another contains a passage which has an almost exact prototype in Bernard of Clairvaux;[86]—when in addition to these facts we remember that the homilies were composed by different men at different times, it seems reasonable to believe that the homilies are, in most cases, compilations brought together from both early and late English and Latin sources, with frequent interspersing of new matter.

In the collections of homilies previously discussed, the exempla have been a part of these additions. The great sources, such as the works of Jerome, Augustine, and Beda, which, together with the writings of Gregory, furnished the body of mediaeval sermons, contained very few exempla. Even in Gregory's homilies, exempla were confined to a limited number of the *Homiliae in Evangelia.* So the exempla in the Blickling, Aelfric, and Wulfstan collections, were mainly English additions to the classic exposition. But the employment of the type in these collections had not been sufficient to exert much influence upon succeeding literature. Nor was such an influence exerted by the homilies of French writers who may have contributed something to the *Old English Homilies.*[87] Moreover, the stimulus derived from the translation of Gregory's *Dialogues* had become weakened by the lapse of time. If, therefore, exempla were to appear in the *Old English Homilies,* they would apparently be due rather to natural impulse than to tradition or external influence.

[83] *O. E. H. First Series,* 122; cf. Thorpe's *Aelfric,* I, 217.

[84] *Ibid., Second Series,* 110; cf. Vollhardt, *op. cit.,* 16.

[85] For example, the following denunciation of contemporary priests: "The layman honoreth his spouse with clothes more than himself, and the priest not so his church, which is his spouse, but adorns his servant, who is his whore, with clothes more than himself. The church cloths are utterly rent and old, and his woman's must be whole and new. His altar cloth coarse and soiled, and her chemise fine and white." *O. E. H., Sec. Ser.,* 162.

[86] See Vollhardt, *op. cit.,* 13.

[87] See Lecoy de la Marche, *La Chaire française,* 11.

A study of these homilies reveals but slight traces of exempla. A few Biblical narratives are used, among them certain parables, which are called "examples." The homily De Natale Domini, for instance, begins, "Godalmihti seiþ an forbisne to his folk in þe halie godspel and seiþ;"[88] then follows the parable of the Good Samaritan, and after it comes a symbolical explanation of the main elements. Such narratives are recounted, not as exempla, but as bases for exposition, frequently symbolical. Cases might also be pointed out in which Biblical persons, such as Moses, Solomon, Job, Mary, and David, are spoken of as examples. Mention should also be made of a small number of curious narrative bits which are told for their historical rather than their illustrative significance.[89] But the exemplum is wanting; its place is supplied by a copious use of figures of speech, analogies, and occasional illustrations from bestiaries,—features which are more effective than the more cumbrous exempla for the clarification of many detailed points.

Whereas the main aim of the Wulfstan homilies is to exhort and secondarily to explain, the reverse is true of the present collection. Symbolism, which seems to have increased in favor, is the chief means of exposition. Closely akin to this method is the use of figures of speech and analogies. These had been employed frequently in standard Latin homilies and patristic writings, and to a certain extent in the earlier English homilies. But there is a notable increase here in the amount of attention paid to similes, metaphors, and analogies, some of which are really elaborate. An interesting case in point may be cited. The writer states that men fast for three reasons, which he enumerates; then he adds: "The example (forbisen) of the washerwomen enables us to understand this. Some bear soiled clothing to the water to wash it clean—so fasteth the sinful man to cleanse himself of his foul sins; others bear

---

[88] *O. E. H., First Series,* 79; see also 231, 244; and *Sec. Ser.,* 155.

[89] An account of the rescue of Jeremiah from the miry pit; an account from the Apocalypse, of the fowl which flew down from heaven to earth and back; an account of St. Paul's visit to hell. See *O. E. H., First Series,* 47, 81, 41, resp.

clean clothes to the water to be bleached, so that they may be white—so doth the righteous man to please our Lord Jesus Christ. . . . Another beareth clean clothes and fair and white —so fasteth the holy man, to be high in heaven and to be near our Lord, and for to have perfect bliss with him."[90] Numerous passages of this kind, indicating much naïve ingenuity in illustrating moral and religious observations, might be cited.[91] Equally noteworthy are the bestiary passages and the comparisons of men with animals. The adder, with a jewel in its head, the fox, the wolf, the bear, the lion, great and little fish, are used as symbols of man. Certain men are also likened to an apple, rosy outside but rotted within; to a tree that beareth leaf and blossom but no fruit. A number of the figures belong distinctly to ecclesiastical tradition; such, for example, is the comparison of water quenching fire with almsdeeds quenching sin; or the likening of Christ's entering the Virgin's womb to the sun shining through a glass window.[92] Other illustrations are of a more homely, unpoetic nature. "Who is he that may water the horse that will not drink himself?" asks the homilist. "No more may anyone do good for their souls who in this life would not begin to do good."[93] Again he asks, "How may the physician heal thee whilst the iron sticketh in the wound? Never. Neither canst thou be shriven sufficiently well to please God Almighty, unless thou forsake all thy sins."[94] These analogies are hardly of argumentative force, but undoubtedly they were illuminating to the audiences addressed, and perhaps

[90] *O. E. H., Sec. Ser.*, 56.

[91] *Ibid., First Ser.*, 22, 32, 80, 122, 158; *Sec. Ser.*, 150, 200.

[92] This idea was popular in Old French religious lyrics, and at a later period in Middle English lyrics. The following stanza from the religious lyrics of Jacob Ryman is characteristic:

> "Seint Anselme seith: 'So Criste did pas
> Thurgh Marie myelde, as his wille was,
> As the sonne beame goth thurgh the glas,
> That mayde full of honoure."

Die Gedichte des Franziskaners Jakob Ryman, printed in Herrig's *Archiv*, vol. 89, p. 186; see also pp. 187, 207.

[93] *O. E. H., First Ser.*, 8–10.

[94] *Ibid., First Ser.*, 22.

even convincing. At any rate, like the exempla in the preceding homily collections, they are rarely, if ever, merely decorative, but have a thoroughly utilitarian office. By means of these figures, analogies, and symbolical interpretations, the doctrines of the Church, the commandments, the mass, the paternoster, shrift, penance, and many Biblical passages, are explained. But the writers of the *Old English Homilies* seem to have made little effort to interest and stimulate their audiences. The use of the exemplum, which, as I showed earlier, depended in this group upon natural impulse, is negligible.

The remaining collection, the *Ormulum,* represents the uninspired homiletic literature of England at the close of the twelfth and the opening of the thirteenth century. The considerable fragment extant is but a part of a more ambitious attempt at Scriptural exegesis than had hitherto been made in English.[95] It also exhibits a lower level of literary interest, and is thoroughly in keeping with the decadent state of popular preaching in England at the opening of the thirteenth century.

A glance at the status of the Church at this time helps us to comprehend better the nature of the *Ormulum.* For a long time, as was previously indicated,[96] Norman prelates had controlled Church affairs in England. These dignitaries were, in most cases, thoroughly worldly, interested in their lands, castles, horses, dogs, and little concerned with what their subordinates did for the masses.[97] Vice, misery and disease among the people were appalling; but there were "few priests, and these were frequently but ill-educated to cope with the difficulties of the situation."[98] Whatever they may have done in other matters, it is certain that preaching was at a low ebb. Jessop states the situation as follows: "The observance of

[95] The work undertook a series of homilies for nearly the whole year; only thirty-two are extant.

[96] See above p. 45, note.

[97] The passage previously quoted (p. 46, note) from the *Old English Homilies,* relative to the priest's neglect of his true spouse, the Church, and the attention paid to personal matters of a questionable nature, might apply to such a state of things. On this point see J. J. Jusserand, *A Literary History of the English People,* I, 162.

[98] Father Cuthbert, *The Friars and how they came to England,* introd., 4.

5

Sunday was almost universally neglected. . . . Sermons had become so rare that when Eustace, Abbot of Flai, preached in various places in England in 1200, miracles were said to have ensued as the ordinary effects of his eloquence."[99] It was at this time, during the reign of King John, that England came under an interdict; as a result, the churches were left desolate and in large districts the worship of God came to an end.[100] Such was the religious situation when the *Ormulum* was produced.

In view of the foregoing facts, it is not at all surprising that homiletic literature should have been heavy and uninspiring. In the case of the *Ormulum,* two vital defects are responsible for tediousness. First, the homilies are almost entirely lacking in originality. The writer does not appear to have been abreast of the times even in his borrowing. Although the lighter and more subtle French literary forms were being utilized in general English literature, and later Latin sources had been drawn upon for English homilies, Orm clings to Beda, Gregory, Josephus, and Isidor.[101] Secondly, the borrowed material is treated in a thoroughly hackneyed manner. After opening with a lengthy paraphrase of a Scriptural passage, the writer almost invariably proceeds to give the symbolical significance, often outdoing his predecessors in farfetched explanations. Salt, stones, grass, smoke, an axe, an ox chewing its cud, the calf,[102]—in short every little detail is made to signify some moral or religious phase of human life. Borrowing of antiquated material, therefore, and a mechanical treatment of an over-worked method of exposition, are largely responsible for the dullness of the *Ormulum.*

[99] Rev. Augustus Jessop, *The Coming of the Friars,* 9.

[100] See Jessop, *op. cit.,* 31.

[101] Dr. Gregor Sarrazin sums up his study of the sources of the *Ormulum* as follows: " Das resultat dieser untersuchung ist das folgende: die hauptquelle des Orrmulum ist Beda, daneben sind die homilien Gregors des grossen benutzt, vielleicht auch Josephus' und Isidors schriften. Von einer directen benutzung Augustins, Hieronymus', oder Aelfrics ist dagegen nichts zu entdecken." *Über die Quellen des Orrmulum,* 26.

[102] The way in which Orm carried symbolism to the extent of absurdity is suggested in the following line: " He [Christ] was tacnedd þurrh þe callf; forr he wass uppo rode." *Ormulum,* I, 207.

Orm did not seem to realize the tediousness of his discourses; at any rate he never apologized for it, nor relieved it by illustrations of an entertaining nature. The term "example" (bisen) frequently appears, in connection with some person like St. Paul or Christ,[103] who are spoken of as "good examples"; or in connection with some Biblical narrative which is the subject of discourse.[104] Both of these uses of the term have been noted in the discussion of the *Old English Homilies*. Orm, apparently, had no feeling for the exemplum.

We may now rapidly review the exemplum as it has appeared in English up to the opening of the thirteenth century. It has been found that Biblical exempla were predominant and that the use of illustrative tales was confined to homiletic literature, with the exception of Alfred's translations of Gregory's *Cura Pastoralis* and the *Consolatio Philosophiae* of Boethius. It was in these two works that the exemplum made its first appearance in English literature. In the case of the *Pastoral Care,* the narratives, usually short Biblical passages, were literally translated. In the *Consolatio,* the translator found not only Biblical episodes but also historical and mythological incidents, which he amplified and made more vital, thereby stamping the type with his approval. In addition to this, Alfred was responsible for the chief influence upon exempla during the period,— Bishop Werferth's translation of the *Dialogues* of Gregory.

Although the translation of the *Dialogues* probably antedated somewhat the *Blickling Homilies,* it is very doubtful if the former influenced the latter to any great extent. These homilies contain few exempla; four distinct cases were noted, two of which represent long-lasting themes. With Aelfric's homilies the use of exempla became well marked. Here, besides a considerable number of Biblical narratives, there are an even greater number of non-Biblical tales. The majority of these are taken from Gregory's *Dialogues,* but the *Vitae Patrum,* legends of the Virgin, and Beda's *Ecclesiastical History* are

---

[103] *Ormulum,* I, 183, 194, 230, 279, 315; II, 23, 24, 27, 112, 113, 331. Christ is most often pointed out as an example.

[104] See *ibid.,* I, 226, et passim.

also used. The exempla are, moreover, usually complete narratives, and have, in the main, the conventional features of the type in its flourishing period. In spite of the indications of conventionality, however, the exemplum is here, as elsewhere throughout the period, thoroughly serious and practical.

The writers of the Wulfstan group no doubt took suggestions from their predecessors. Here too, exempla are frequently employed, but the number of Biblical narratives in these homilies outnumbers the non-Biblical. This has been explained as the practical adaptation of convenient and authoritative illustrative matter by zealous reformers who lacked the literary taste of Aelfric. We found that the exempla used by these men, though strikingly forceful, were crude in construction, and in most cases unconventionally treated.

It has been noted that the *Old English Homilies* fell in a period when preaching in England was becoming almost universally neglected. They consist of compilations from early and late English and Latin sources, with some admixture of original passages. None of the sources drawn upon furnished a strong influence for the use of exempla, but each one emphasized symbolical interpretations, figures of speech, and analogies. These were constantly used in the *Old English Homilies* and were, no doubt, better suited than exempla to the detailed explanations which characterize the group. The virtual disappearance of the exemplum from these homilies suggested that the use of illustrative narratives in religious literature might not after all be so obvious and natural a device, but that anything like a systematic use of exempla must be a product of literary tradition, or of a strong immediate influence from without.

This conclusion was strengthened by the absence of exempla from the *Ormulum,* which with its dry, unrelieved paraphrases, and time-worn symbolical expositions, indicates the decadence of English preaching at the close of the twelfth century. The earlier influences which had made for an extensive use of the exemplum had become weakened by the lapse of time, and although it is quite likely that illustrative narratives were occasionally employed, any considerable usage depended upon a revival. Such a revival came, influenced by the growing popularity of saints' lives, and encouraged by the preaching friars. But, as I shall attempt to show in the next chapter, the flourishing period of exempla in the vernacular was preceded in England by a growth of the type in Latin, under the influence of Continental churchmen.

CHAPTER III

The Latin Exemplum in England

We have noted that the use of illustrative tales in English literature to the end of the twelfth century was confined to sermons, and that even there, at the close of that period, such tales were only occasionally employed. The practice had been born of foreign, not native impulse. When the revival of the exemplum came, and use of the type was extended beyond the sermon, foreign influence was again responsible.

As has already been stated, the coming of the friars to England[1] gave a great impulse to the popularization of moral and religious literature, but before that time the exemplum in England was spreading in the Latin works of men who had mingled with Continental churchmen. Those curious miscellanies of the twelfth century, such as John of Salisbury's *Polycraticus,* Walter Map's *De Nugis Curialium,* and Gervase of Tilbury's *Otia Imperialia,* were preparing for the later vogue of illustrative tales. A little later, in the last quarter of the twelfth century, Alexander Neckam's *De Naturis Rerum* employs them, and at the opening of the thirteenth century, Giraldus Cambrensis in his *Gemma Ecclesiastica* makes so copious a use of monkish tales that the work is really an example-book. Finally, in the Latin sermons of Odo de Ceritona, which were written before 1219,[2] exempla are strikingly prominent. These representative writers were men who had lived and studied on the Continent, especially in France,[3] and had imbibed the clerical taste for illustrative tales and fables, which were circulating among Continental churchmen.

John of Salisbury's *Polycraticus,* or *De Nugis Curialium,*[4]

[1] The Dominicans came in 1221, and the Franciscans in 1224.

[2] See Hervieux, *Les Fabulistes,* IV, 46.

[3] It will be remembered that the "English Nation" was famous in the University of Paris during the twelfth century.

[4] Edited by Migne, *Patr. Lat.,* CXCIX.

written shortly after the middle of the twelfth century, consists of eight books which, in treating of the nature of men and affairs, are replete with illustrative incidents from Greek and Roman history and mythology, the *Bible,* the Latin poets, and widely scattered historical gleanings. Often a story of considerable length is used to illustrate a general observation. For instance, after speaking generally about the extremes to which hunger will reduce people, John of Salisbury says, " Sed quid opus est per haec pondus famis illius explicare cum gestum sit ibi facinus, quod neque apud Graecos, neque apud barbaros, ullus accepit auditus?" Then he relates a story of a woman who, driven to desperation by hunger, ate her own son.[5] Again, the writer maintains that flatterers should be punished, and in illustration of various phases of the subject he cites episodes from the lives of Aristippus, Metellus, Xenophon, Diogenes, Alexander, Caesar, and others.[6] In another place he makes his point concrete by recalling an incident which occurred during the reign of Edward the Confessor.[7] The episode of Brennus from Roman History[8] is another representative illustration, typical of the matter in this curious mosaic of general observation, learning, and narrative. The exempla are comparatively few and briefly told, but they show that the type existed in the Latin literature of the time.

Walter Map's *De Nugis Curialium* is similar in general plan to its more serious forerunner of the same title. It was written considerably later, however, probably between 1182–89,[9] and is much richer in monkish anecdotes and legendary tales. These are scattered through the five "Distinctiones" into which the treatise is divided. A brief outline of the sections may be useful. (1) Map compares the English court to the infernal regions, drawing pictures of such persons as Tantalus and Sisyphus; narrates stories of the follies and crimes of the court; tells monastic tales; gives accounts of the origins of

[5] *Polycraticus,* 423.

[6] *Ibid.,* 506.

[7] *Ibid.,* 598.

[8] *Ibid.,* 612.

[9] *Gualteri Mapes De Nugis Curialium,* preface, ix–x.

monkish orders, Templars, and Hospitallers, with reflections on their corruption; attacks the Cistercians; discusses various heretical sects; and closes with a tale of three hermits. (2) The second opens with tales of pious monks and hermits and their miracles; then follow some anecdotes illustrative of Welsh manners; the section closes with a collection of curious fairy legends. (3) The third consists of four fairly long stories of a romantic nature: *de societate Sadii et Galonis, de contrarietate Parii et Lausi, de Ransone et ejus uxore, de Rollone et ejus uxore.* (4) The fourth contains the *Dissuasio Valerii ad Rufinum philosophum ne uxorem ducat,* and a number of tales and legends of both popular and historical interest. (5) The last section consists of several English historical traditions dealing with Earl Godwin and Cnut, and a sketch of the English court from the reign of William Rufus to that of Henry II. The work was avowedly written to show the strenuous and involved existence of a courtier,[10] but how seldom the writer strayed into that particular field may be judged by a glance over the foregoing outline.

The book has for us a special interest, not merely because it uses illustrative tales, but also because it shows thus early in England the tendency to collect monkish stories, which were evidently already circulating among churchmen, and to compile other legendary incidents which were to furnish stock in trade for the preachers and moralists of a later day. The following exemplum, which Map uses to illustrate the constancy of the early Templars, is typical of the monkish legends in his treatise.

" Quiddam Mirabile

Circa tempus idem, clericus quidam a Sarracenis sagittabatur ut negaret. Quidam autem qui negaverat astans inproperabat ei quod stulte crederet, et ad singulos ictus aiebat, ‘ Estne bonum ? ’ Ille nihil contra. Cumque videret ejus constantiam, uno sibi caput amputavit ictu, dicens, ‘ Estne bonum ? ’ Caput autem resectum cum proprio ore loquens intulit, ‘ Nunc bonum est.’ ”

Map then continues : " Haec et his similia primitis contigerunt Templaribus, dum Domini caritas et mundi vilitas inerat. Ut autem caritas viluit, et invaluit opulentia, prorsus alias audi-

---

[10] *De Nugis Curialium,* preface, x.

vimus quas et subjiciemus fabulas; at et prius eorum primos a paupertate motus audiantur."[11]   Immediately following this is another tale which relates how a certain knight named Hamericus set out for a tournament, but hearing the morning bell of a religious house he parted from his companions to hear mass, thinking to follow them shortly.   After mass he unwittingly strays into a by-path which brings him at night back to the place of worship.   This is repeated on the next day.   On the third day a hermit guides him to his companions, who joyously greet him with congratulations.   He is much surprised and suspects ridicule.   Upon calling aside a close friend, however, he learns that the enemy has been turned back because of their wonder at his own prowess.   He then comprehends that a miracle has been wrought and that divine service has accomplished more than feats of arms, so he thereafter devotes himself and his possessions to the service of God and the Templars.[12]

Among other incidents relating to holy men, the second section contains six accounts of apparitions and four of prodigies, all of the last involving moral or religious situations.   One of them, for example, which appears in the so-called *Chronicle of Turpin*, tells of a man who left his goods to a cleric with directions to distribute them among the poor.   But the cleric failed in his duty and was warned that at a certain time he would be snatched into the air by demons.   Although he surrounded himself by a great army of soldiers, at the stated time he was torn away into the air and later dashed to pieces on the rocks.[13]

A number of the legends in the third section are common in mediaeval exemplum collections; the following are typical themes: a prodigal young man is restored to fortune by making a compact with the devil; a man disregards three warnings of death and meets a terrible fate; a pious painter meets with favor at the hands of the Virgin.[14]   Map rarely drew the moral

---

[11] *De Nugis Curialium*, 31.

[12] *Ibid.*, 31.

[13] *De Nugis Curialium*, 105.

[14] *Ibid.*, 154–5–6.   Cf. Wright's *Latin Stories*, 13, 34, 35, resp.   The Three Warnings of Death appears in Bromyard's *Summa Praedicantium*, under the title, "Mors."

in connection with his tales, but being a churchman he no doubt anticipated their beneficial effects.

The *Otia Imperialia*,[15] a work of a younger contemporary of Map, Gervase of Tilbury, should be mentioned here, not because it is rich in exempla, but because it further indicates the vogue of corrective, entertaining and instructive miscellanies. The list of sources drawn upon for this work numbers seventy-five items.[16] It was written, according to J. A. Sandys, about 1211, for the amusement of the German Emperor, Otto IV;[17] at any rate, it is calculated to entertain and instruct rather than to reform. An occasional tale, such as No. XVIII, "De visione portarum inferni," or No. CXXIX, "De fonte, qui nihil sordidum admittit," might well be used to point a moral. But the work consists almost wholly in descriptions and accounts of natural phenomena and wonders of the world.

Alexander Neckam's similar and slightly earlier work, *De Naturis Rerum,* makes considerable use of exempla. This book, it would appear from John of Bromton's *Chronicle,* was well known at the end of the twelfth century.[18] Neckam, like the other writers mentioned in this chapter, had been in contact with foreign scholars and churchmen; in fact, he was for a time a professor in the University of Paris.[19] Later, he held an ecclesiastical office in England until his death in 1217.

De Naturis Rerum is, as may be remembered, a compilation from such sources as Solinus, Cassiodorus, Aristotle, Pliny, Vergil, Lucan, Martial, Bernard Silvester, Ovid, Boethius, St. Augustine, Juvenal, the *Bible,* ancient history, traditions, mythology, and contemporary superstitions. Of particular significance for the present investigation is the use to which exempla are put to explain and illustrate the nature of animals and natural phenomena. Neckam's scholarly pursuits and clerical learning had brought him into contact with exempla,

[15] *Des Gervasius von Tilbury Otia Imperialia, in einer Auswahl neu herausgegeben,* Felix Liebrecht, Hannover, 1856.

[16] *Ibid.,* preface, xi–xii, note.

[17] *Cambridge History of English Literature,* I, 213.

[18] See *De Naturis Rerum,* preface, xiii–xiv.

[19] *Ibid.,* preface, x.

which, as I have shown, were already circulating. These
enabled him to add a number of excellent moral touches to his
treatise,—an addition which no true mediaeval writer would
forego.

The exempla, though not very numerous, are of no little importance in that they appear in a treatise on natural history.
I shall cite only the more important ones, which show Neckam's
purpose in introducing them, and represent the kinds of tales
employed. After speaking about the dangers of the sea and
the bravery of sailors, he illustrates and confirms the discussion by telling a story, on the authority of eye-witnesses,[20] of
a man who used to cross the "mare Britannicum" with only
his dog to help him. In another place he illustrates the nobility
of the horse by narrating how Broiefort aided his master Ogier
the Dane in conquering the Saracens at the siege of Meaux.[21]
A marginal note opposite this tale runs, "De commedatione
equorum et exemplum de Ogero." In some cases he draws a
moral (instructio moralis) after the narrative. For example,
he writes that the birds once assembled to choose a king, and
decided to confer that honor upon that bird which should fly
highest. The wren hid under the eagle's wing and just as the
latter was about to claim the award, the wren hopped upon the
head of the rightful victor.[22] This little tale, Neckam points
out at some length, shows how some people wrongfully rise to
high honors and rewards by the labors of others. The
moralist supplants the naturalist.

None of the tales above mentioned are common in collections
of exempla, but certain others appear again and again in later
compilations. There are three of these: (1) the knight and
the lion. In Neckam's version the knight rescues the lion from
a serpent and in order to escape from the grateful beast's
companionship he betakes himself to the sea; the lion tries to
follow and is drowned.[23] This tale, he points out, exemplifies

[20] *De Naturis Rerum*, 141. "Relatu eorum qui testimonium de visu
perhibuerunt."
[21] *Ibid.*, 261.
[22] *Ibid.*, 122.
[23] *Ibid.*, 229.

gratitude. (2) The knight and his three sons. A noble knight with a depraved wife had three sons. Shortly before his death he called his feudal lord and asked him to select one of his sons as his successor. After the knight's death, the lord, realizing the infidelity of the wife, determined to make a test which would discover to him the true son. He therefore proposed to the boys that they find who can inflict the deepest wound upon the dead body of their father. Two of the supposed sons made their most powerful thrusts but the third refused to compete in the mutilation of his father's body; he was selected as the lawful heir.[24] (3) The fate of a glutton. The Count of Pons-Ysarae was a good man except for gluttony. One day after his death, his virtuous son with a party of friends visited the Count's tomb. Upon removing the top, they found a loathsome toad clinging to the neck through which so much rich food had passed.[25] Much moralizing follows this tale, which, like the other two, was a favorite with later teachers of right-living. The appearance of exempla in this secular compendium is of considerable importance in indicating their presence and favor among the Latin writers at the close of the twelfth century.

The next work which we shall consider deals with a subject more closely related to exempla. It is the *Gemma Ecclesiastica*[26] of the influential churchman, Giraldus Cambrensis. The book was probably written at Lincoln between 1196–99[27] and was presented by the author to Pope Innocent III who was implored by bishops and cardinals for a loan of the manuscript. The Pope valued it so highly, however, that he would not let it be taken away.[28] This much-treasured work was a treatise on the sacraments of the Church, ecclesiastical abuses, and matters pertaining to clerical discipline, interspersed with a great number of exempla. Giraldus' introductory words to the

[24] *De Naturis Rerum*, 313.

[25] *Ibid.*, 334.

[26] *Giraldi Cambrensis Opera*, II.

[27] See *ibid.*, VII, 168.

[28] *Gemma*, Brewer's preface, ix–x.

clergy are so suggestive of the status of exempla at the time that I venture to quote at some length.

"It is not altogether undeserving of your praise and gratitude, that out of ponderous volumes, where, owing to the diffuseness of the authors, it is not easy to find what is more worthy and elegant, I have collected into a small compass all that savored of sounder sense and was more adapted to your spiritual weal, and have made a compendium out of the waste and luxuriance of other men. My task is that of the man who from the innumerable sands on the seashore picks out with much labor the precious gems; or who selects as he walks through spacious gardens from the foolish and fruitless herbs the useful and the virtuous, separating the lilies and roses from the nettles and brambles."

"The subject of my book falls under two heads, one of precept, the other of example. For, as Jerome tells us: 'Long and tedious is the way that leads by precept; commodious and brief is the way that leads by example.'[29] So, from the legends of the holy Fathers, of which very few copies are to be found among you of Wales, and from the faithful narratives of ancient and of more recent times, I have compiled, with a view to your imitation, some things which will be not unserviceable to you. To the words of instruction I have subjoined examples in suitable places, that as from the perusal of the former you may gain learning, from the latter you may derive consolation and be provoked to emulation."

"I am well aware, that to learned ears and fastidious readers, to whom all these things are trite and common, my work will appear either tedious or superfluous. But I would have such men understand that this work is intended exclusively for my own country of Wales; and it is therefore set forth in phrase and matter intelligible and unrefined, without rhetorical ornament. I aim at being perspicuous, no more. But if, perchance, this work of mine, transgressing the limits prescribed to it, should flit across the Marches, fall into the hands of great ones, and presumptuously intrude upon the eyes of the learned, let such readers know that I prefer to set before them what they may consider superfluous than to withhold from my countrymen what I deem to be necessary."[30]

The fact that Giraldus, when seeking advancement, chose a copy of this book rather than anything else to present to the great Innocent III, suggests that the apology was conventional,

[29] The term "examples" here, as with Gregory, the Knight of La Tour Landry (see above, pp. 11, 14, resp.), and others, seems to refer to the actual deeds of men, but unquestionably these writers had in mind the narrations of such deeds, since they invariably proceed to cite exempla.

[30] *Gemma*, xi–xii. I have used the editor's translation of this passage, making a change in the last sentence of the second paragraph where he interchanged "former" and "latter."

rather than sincere.[31]   However that may be, his statements as to the method of selecting these "precious gems" from the "innumerable sands," his implication that at least a "very few copies" of the patristic legends could be found even in Wales at the time, his recommendation of the serviceableness of exempla, are pertinent observations on the presence and favor of the type among the learned at the opening of the thirteenth century.

We may now turn to the book itself, which is divided into two parts.   The first treats in a familiar manner of matters, small and great, which presented everyday problems to the clergy, such as the administration of the eucharist, extreme unction, the mass, confession, the ornamentation of the church, the enjoining of penance, and kindred topics.   The second part deals with matters of conduct and of contemporary clerical abuses.   In both parts a voluminous mass of tales and anecdotes is used to illustrate and confirm the text; twenty-eight anecdotes,[32] for instance, support the single point of ignorance among the clergy.   Giraldus takes his narratives from a variety of sources, such as the *Vitae Patrum,* the *Dialogues* of Gregory, saints' lives, and historical compends;[33] but what distinguishes the exempla particularly is the number of contemporary instances of which the writer either knew directly or had heard.   These not only add to the charm of the treatise but must also have increased its convincing quality.

Practically the whole body of illustrations deals with ecclesiastical affairs.   The use of purely secular incidents is a later tendency in the history of the exemplum.   In order to indicate the tone which pervades the narratives, I give herewith a few themes taken almost at random.   After speaking of the value and sanctity of the eucharist, the writer recalls four incidents which are in substance as follows: Maurice, Bishop of Paris, reproved the Canons of St. Victor for offering him on his death-bed unconsecrated wafers, in the belief that he was too

[31] He also presented a copy to the Lincoln Cathedral Library; see ed. cit., VII, 168.

[32] *Gemma,* 341 seq.

[33] It is to be noted that Biblical exempla were less and less frequently employed as monkish tales multiplied and became more available.

far gone to realize the deception.[34]   The writer saw in Paris
an Englishman, Richard de Aubry, who was unable on his
death-bed to take into his mouth the viaticum because he had
not believed in transubstantiation.[35]   At the suggestion of the
devil, a woman waited to take from the mouth of the dying
Urban III the viaticum which he had been unable to swallow.[36]
Pope Gerbert, when he should have held up the host in the
service, used to turn his back to the audience and drop the
burden into a sack suspended from his neck.   When he con-
fessed to this deception, a rule was made requiring the pope to
face the audience when he officiated.   Gerbert, in penitence
for this and other offences of his early life, mutilated himself.
It is said that in consequence of this his marble tomb sweats
blood at the impending death of the reigning pontiff.[37]   Brief
anecdotes of this kind are sprinkled plentifully through the
book.

   Besides such colorless stories, there are a considerable number which, though told in a serious manner and with a serious
purpose, are pleasantly absurd.   For instance, in connection
with transubstantiation, Giraldus tells of a contemporary German who for some reason put the pix in a hollow tree.   Later
it was found surrounded by a little ornamented wax temple
which the bees had made for it.[38]   The lesson of honoring the
holy paraphernalia is clear and would no doubt sink deep into
the hearts of a thirteenth century audience.   It is quite probable that Giraldus himself was not altogether incredulous of
some of the strange accounts that came to his notice.[39]   For
example, he states that he has heard it for a fact—" Ego etiam
de quodam verissime audivi "—that a man who had unwittingly
swallowed a spider in the sacramental wine was relieved three

[34] *Gemma,* 32.
[35] *Ibid.,* 33.
[36] *Ibid.,* 34.
[37] *Ibid.,* 34.
[38] *Ibid.,* 42.
[39] J. F. Dimock, in his preface to the *Topographia Hibernica* (ed. cit., V.
lxvii), says, " He [Giraldus] was almost as credulous as he was vain and
pompous, exactly the man that a joker would fix upon as fair and first-rate
game."

days later by scratching the offending creature out of his great toe.[40] I may cite another instance of his tendency to believe strange tales, especially when they came or were supposed to come from high authority. He relates, on the authority of Bishop Baldwin of Worcester, a case of a young woman who proffered love to a young man. The latter, suspicious of an evil spirit, made certain tests but still was not satisfied. The woman became impatient and one day, seeing him pay more attention to a hound named Galiena than to herself, left him with the words, "'You have slighted me for Galiena; Galiena shall avenge me for this affront.'" Later the young man met and fell desperately in love with a girl named Galiena who consistently repulsed him. Despite his efforts to forget her by retiring to a monastery, despite the prayers of the brothers, he died of unrequited love.[41] The outcome of the story was at variance with the usual reward for withstanding temptation and the narrator was at loss to explain the affair. As Brewer says, "The reflections of Giraldus on this occasion show the perplexity under which he labored. It never occurred to him to question the authenticity of the narrative, nor could he for a moment doubt the authority on which he had received it."[42]

But if Giraldus was strangely credulous, he was not a wilful impostor, as is shown by a statement in the *Topographia Hibernica,* relative to those wonderful anecdotes and marvelous monstrosities there recorded. He says that he does not desire that credence should be given to all that has been advanced in the chapter on the marvels and miracles of Ireland, inasmuch as he dares not himself believe those things unless they have actually fallen within his own observation, or might so have fallen. As for the rest, he forbears to pronounce upon them affirmatively or negatively, but leaves them rather to the reader's judgment.[43] Giraldus, in common with the majority of mediaeval clerics, accepted and recounted many unplausible tales as gospel fact, but the probability is that in the eagerness to establish the principles exemplified, the reality or fictitiousness of the concrete instance was often forgotten.

[40] *Gemma,* 122.
[41] *Ibid.,* 228.
[42] *Ibid.,* introd., 50
[43] Ed. cit., V, 74–5.

Closely akin to Giraldus' narration of incredible happenings is his use of trivial, ridiculously incongruous illustrations. This is a charge which may also be brought against many mediaeval preachers and moralists who employed exempla. It might be expected, nevertheless, that a man who in his observations on the conduct of Church affairs shows such remarkable moderation and good sense, would have exercised more discrimination. Its absence we can interpret only as another manifestation of the mediaeval fondness for the juxtaposition of incongruities. As an illustration of the trivial anecdotes employed as exempla in the *Gemma* I shall quote two of the four which are used to show the terrific effects of excommunication. In each case the unfortunate subjects of this mighty weapon of the Church are vermin!

" Exemplum de beato Bernardo abbate Clarevallensi, qui cum ad ecclesiam quandam venisset, sicut in legenda ipsius reperitur, in qua, propter muscarum ingruentem abundantiam, nec etiam divina celebrari poterant, et hoc ei referretur; subjecit vir sanctus: ' Et ego in nomine Christi eas excommunico.' Mane vero omnes, tam in ecclesia quam per claustra domus et septa, mortuae inventae sunt."

" Item exemplum de sancto Yvoro episcopo, qui majores mures, qui vulgariter *rati* vocantur, quia libros suos forte eroderant, per suam imprecationem a provincia Hiberniae, quae Fernegulam dicitur, in qua deliquerant, prorsus ejecit, adeo ut nec ibi postea longo tempore nasci, nec vivere valeant advecti."[44]

The appearance of such pied-piper accounts is not at all uncommon in this book of grave and sound observations on the greatest of mediaeval institutions.

For the most part Giraldus' exempla are neither more trivial nor more serious than those employed by other men during the centuries immediately following. Stories relating the deplorable acts of evil spirits and devils,[45] and tales illustrative of the worldliness, impurity, avarice and ignorance of the contemporary clergy, abound.[46] As is usual wherever any appre-

[44] *Gemma,* 160–61.
[45] *Ibid.,* 53, 54, 55, 56, 158, 260, passim.
[46] Two typical illustrations of the latter class are in substance as follows. A priest in speaking about Barnabas told his audience that he was a good man but yet he was a thief for the gospels say, " ' erat autem Barabbas latro ' "; the priest made no distinction between Barnabas and Barabbas.

ciable use of exempla is made, the work includes a few stock favorites.[47] The incidents, though usually short and unadorned, are at times very brisk and entertaining. This is particularly true of those which deal with Giraldus' personal observation. As a whole, this treatise and example-book is not only unusually interesting, but since it was addressed to the clergy by so prominent a man, it must have had considerable influence for the encouragement of our type.

Of equal or even greater importance was the work of the English preacher and fable writer, Odo de Ceritona.[48] His collection of fables and tales, compiled between 1219–21, is apparently the earliest in which fables are accompanied with moralizations. Although preachers used this collection as a source-book for illustrations, it was probably compiled to reform clerical abuses. Those "parabolae" which were intended for exempla, Odo inserted in his sermons but never collected.[49] The collected narratives, by virtue of their accompanying moralizations, acquired a greater independent value than they had hitherto possessed in the subordinate office of illustrations. The collection was composed largely of fables, but the idea of appending moralizations was soon applied to collections of tales other than fables and helped to produce such compilations as the *Gesta Romanorum*. These moralized tales and fables of Odo were eagerly utilized by preachers[50] who in copying them

Another instance of the same kind tells of a priest who in a sermon on the woman of Canaan, said that she was part woman and part dog, "inter Cananeam et caninam non bene distinguens." *Gemma*, 341.

[47] It is worthy of notice that Giraldus relates the tale, immortalized by Cervantes, of a man hiding money in a cane which he has his creditor hold while he swears that he has paid his debt.

[48] *Les Fabulistes Latins*, IV, contains the fables and parables of Odo, and a thorough critical and biographical study of their author.

[49] See Hervieux, *Les Fabulistes*, IV, 35.

[50] That some of Odo's contemporaries were using exempla is evinced by sermon collections still preserved. Wright calls attention to some of them as follows. "In a manuscript [Arundel, 231] . . . in the British Museum some monastic compiler has arranged in one series the homilies of John of Abbeville, Odo of Kent, and Roger of Salisbury on the Sunday Gospels throughout the year. . . They all present one characteristic which is much less common in the writers of sermons at an early date, the frequent illus-

into collections for their own use "sometimes lengthened, shortened, or otherwise changed them, sometimes added others, borrowed, in theme at least, from other authors or from their own imagination."[51] The large number of manuscripts containing such collections still extant in France, Germany, England, Belgium, Italy, and Switzerland,[52] testify amply to the popularity of Odo's fables.[53]

The fables, however, though often mingled in the sermons as exempla,[54] are of less importance for our study than the "parabolae," or exempla, which appeared in his sermons, written previous to 1219.[55] There are two collections of homilies: those for Sundays (Homiliae de Tempore), and those for Festivals (Homiliae de Sanctis). Of the former there are sixty-six; of the latter, twenty-six. The exempla in these sermons show growing familiarity with such writers as Seneca, Ovid, Vergil, Horace, Juvenal, Claudian, and Boethius.[56] Moreover, the type is employed on a scale far greater than in any of the English homily collections of the earlier period. Hervieux' edition of the "parabolae" used in the Sunday sermons only, contains one hundred and ninety-nine.

Odo's chief sources for exempla, outside of fables and traditional anecdotes, are Gregory's *Dialogues* and the *Vitae Patrum*. The *Bible* and secular history are sparingly utilized;

tration of the subject by short stories or fables." *Biographia Britannica Literaria*, I, 225. The *Catalogue of the Western MSS. in Trinity College* lists (I, 9–11) a thirteenth century MS. of fifty-nine "Sermones per anni circulum," which formerly belonged to the Durham Cathedral. Mr. James, the compiler of the catalogue, notes that stories are used in many of these sermons.

[51] Hervieux, *op. cit.*, IV, 35.

[52] *Ibid.*, IV, 47–77.

[53] Hervieux states that there are only three translations of Odo's fables: One Spanish (*El libro de los gatos*), and two French. One of the latter is anonymous; the other he believes to be the *Contes Moralisés* of Nicole de Bozon. *Les Fabulistes*, IV, 85.

[54] Seventeen of the Aesopic collection appear in the homilies, besides nine others "au moins en germe." *Ibid.*, IV, 124–5.

[55] *Ibid.*, IV, 46.

[56] *Ibid.*, IV, 126.

Latin classics and patristic writings are more frequently cited.
Compared with the illustrative tales previously discussed in
this chapter, those of the present collection show a more constant and serious aim to exemplify and correct the sins and
weaknesses of the masses.[56a] Most of the exempla in the
sermons are followed, as were the fables, by a clear application to the condition of the audience. "Sic ergo faciat
Domine," "Ita in presentia," "Huius modi," "Similiter,"
"Tales sunt cupidi," are expressions indicative of the usual
manner in which Odo introduces his moralizations from the
tales. Sometimes the moralization takes the form of a symbolical interpretation, of which I shall give illustration later.

The exempla used by Odo may be classified under the following heads: (1) historical incidents, (2) Biblical narratives,
(3) fables, (4) Bestiary passages and figures of speech,[57]
(5) monkish tales. The first four groups I shall consider
briefly before passing to the monkish tales, which comprise
fully two-thirds of the entire number. The historical group
consists of about half a dozen incidents, such as the death of
Julian the Apostate at the hands of a special agent of the
Virgin,[58] the account of Socrates hurling a great lump of gold
into the sea with the observation that one cannot possess riches
and virtue,[59] the inability of Canute to keep back the sea.[60]
Most of these are vague and legendary rather than authentic.
The Biblical exempla, of which there are about the same
number, are for the most part mere references. For instance,
one of them consists of a single line, " Paulus post naufragium
a vipere percussus est; nihil ei nocuit."[61] The moralization
occupies four lines. Another, which I translate entire, is but

---

[56a] Hervieux remarks that Odo "avait un grand amour de la pureté."
Les Fabulistes, IV, 29.

[57] That Odo considered bestiary passages and figures of speech in much
the same light as exempla is suggested by his definition of "parabolæ":
" Parabola dicitur a *para,* quod est juxta, et *bole,* quod est sententia, quasi
juxta sententiam. Parabola enim est similitudo quae ponitur ad sententiam
rei comprobandam." *Les Fabulistes,* 110.

[58] *Les Fabulistes,* IV, 271.

[59] *Ibid.,* 271.

[60] *Ibid.,* 275.

[61] *Ibid.,* 299.

little longer: "It is said that Dives, tired of the clamor of the beggar, set his dogs on him. But the dogs licked his wounds."[62] Elijah under the juniper tree occupies three lines.[63] The episode of the citizens of Ephesus who turned back from following Paul seemed particularly worthy to the homilist since it is given no less than a page and a quarter.[64] Among the bestiary passages may be found references to the pelican and its young,[65] the elephant's habit of leaning against a tree which the hunter cuts,[66] the antelope caught among the branches by its spreading antlers.[67] These, and a few references to the habits of the hen which gathers its chicks, the fly which pollutes, and the wolf which feigns death, are used to symbolize human qualities. They are hardly more than figures of speech. The Aesopic fables incorporated in the sermons are of greater significance both in number and bulk, but they offer no special object for discussion, so we may turn to the group of greatest importance, the monkish legends.

A large number of these are of the familiar, clerical, unlocalized kind, dealing with "a certain rustic," "a certain king," "a certain bishop," or "a certain hermit." The following outlines will indicate their simple and homely character. A certain rustic who was invited by his lord to a feast, drank putrid water from a ditch outside his lord's dwelling, in spite of the remonstrances of his companion. Later, in the midst of the company, he vomited the putrid water upon the table. Then follows Odo's moralization that in the present, men spoil their lives by evil-doing and only by penance may they fit themselves to partake of the heavenly feast.[68] A certain great nobleman, having relinquished the pomp of the world and taken the habit of the white monks, was asked why he had done such a thing. He replied that he judged it better to gain salvation in vile clothes than to perish in silken stuff.[69] In others of

[62] *Les Fabulistes,* IV, 305.

[63] *Ibid.,* 322.

[64] *Ibid.,* 339–40.

[65] *Ibid.,* 269.

[66] *Ibid.,* 316.

[67] *Ibid.,* 327.

[68] *Ibid.,* 266.

[69] *Ibid.,* 268.

this kind, the moral is drawn on a detailed allegorical basis. For example, a certain man had a beautiful wife whom he often spurned and afflicted; but his vicious maid-servant he nourished and fed with delicacies. The wife is the soul which we misuse; the servant is the flesh which we pamper and indulge.[70]

Other monkish tales deal with incidents in the lives of particular saints, such as St. Anthony, St. Lawrence, St. Hilary, St. Martin, and St. Machary. Legends about devils and reappearances after death are prominent. The monkish group contains also a limited number combating abuses among the clergy. For example, a Master of Paris asserted that Peter and Paul were fools, and upon being questioned, explained that they suffered poverty, toil and hunger to be saved, whereas present-day bishops were able to win salvation with rich food and drink, fine clothes and luxuries.[71] A very amusing tale of this class satirizes the greed of churchmen. A little old woman (vetula) not being able to get a hearing from the bishop, was advised by one who knew his custom, not to attempt to importune that dignitary until she had annointed his palm. The woman, interpreting this advice in a very simple manner, straightway secured three pieces of butter and sought the bishop. At her request he stretched out his hand which she suddenly greased well with the rich butter. Odo's comment is brief but pertinent, "Utinam tale obsequium omnibus cupidis exhiberetur."[72] The foregoing exempla are perpetuated in subsequent collections, as are the following, which I outline briefly because they are thoroughly typical of the themes constantly appearing in the great collections of exempla.

(1) "De Juliano apostata et diabolo." This relates how Julian sent a demon on a wicked errand, but the demon was stopped and turned back by chancing to fly above a certain religious man who prayed day and night.[73]

(2) "De sene cui angelus judicia dei ostendit." This story,

---

[70] *Les Fabulistes*, IV, 270.

[71] *Ibid.*, 268.

[72] *Ibid.*, 301.

[73] *Ibid.*, 296–7.

the theme of Parnell's *Hermit,* tells of an angel who stole a gold cup from a generous host, later gave the stolen cup to a miserly host, and finally strangled the infant child of a pious host. The agent of God then explained to his revolted mortal companion just how he was executing God's wisdom in doing these apparently atrocious things.[74]

(3) "De quodam eremita et cadavere fetente." An angel traveling along the roadside with a hermit, passed by a rotting corpse, unnoticing, but held his nose at the sight of a fashionably arrayed young gentleman.[75]

(4) "De quodam monacho et patre ejus." This is one of the many variants of an extremely popular theme,—the heroic struggles of clerics to withstand temptations, usually contrived by the devil. A young monk upon being solicited by a woman, consults his father, who advises forty days' labor on bread and water. After twenty days the devil in the guise of a revolting Ethiopian female appears to the youth and states that it was she who had been his former charming temptress. The youth and his father render thanks to God, but the father remarks that if the son had stayed in the hermitage for the rest of the forty days, he would have perceived the deception even more clearly.[76]

(5) "De quadam sancta religiosa." This anecdote tells of a girl whose father was ever heavy and sad, whereas her mother was proud, talkative and lustful. After their death, the girl in a vision saw their respective dwellings in the other world; the father in bliss, the mother in hell-torment.[77]

(6) "De quodam clerico flente et abbate Bernardo." A penitent young cleric wrote a list of his sins on a card which he sent to Bernard. When the abbot looked at the card, the writing, owing to God's mercy to penitents, had disappeared.

[74] *Les Fabulistes,* IV, 308.

[75] *Ibid.,* 275.

[76] *Ibid.,* 329–30.

[77] *Ibid.,* 330–2. The frequent appearance of this theme in mediaeval writings, indicates that the doctrine that sadness in this life brought happiness in the next, and vice versa, was not only held by ascetics but was taught to the masses.

So, through confession, the card of the heart is wiped clean of the letters of sin, runs the allegorical moral.[78]

All of these exempla are brief,[79] tersely phrased, and usually obvious in their lessons of faith, reward for good, or punishment for evil actions. A clerical preference for the incidents recorded in the works of the Church Fathers, the *Dialogues* of Gregory, the *Vitae Patrum,* and saints' lives, is to be noted. Hervieux has suggested that Odo told these tales to the people as actual facts rather than as legendary illustrations. That he, like Giraldus, may have considered the incidents for the most part factual is not at all unlikely, inasmuch as he takes pains occasionally to caution his audience that a certain account is not quite authentic.[80] The faith in the substance of exempla, the belief in their efficacy,[81] their prominence, and the fact that the manuscripts of Odo's sermons are plentiful,[82] are all indications that the type was growing in favor among contemporary scholars and churchmen.[83]

We have seen in the work of these Latin writers of England in the second half of the twelfth century, that narratives were already becoming important as illustrations. This is evident

[78] *Les Fabulistes,* IV, 336–7.

[79] The average length of the exempla in the collection is about nine lines.

[80] For example, he introduces the tale about the weeping child who was cured by bathing where Christ had bathed, with the words, " Dicitur, licet non sit autenticum." *Les Fabulistes,* IV, 330. Hervieux cites (ibid., 112) another case which closes with the words, " Sed non est autenticum."

[81] Among other things, Odo says in one of his prologues, " Paterfamilias debet proferre de thesauro suo nova et vetera verba et exempla, quibus reficiatur fidelis anima." A little later he refers to the authority of Gregory, as follows: " Et quoniam, ut dicit Gregorius, plus quandoque compungunt exempla quam verba; aperiam in parabolis os meum, et similitudines et exempla que libencius audiuntur, memorie firmius quam verba commendantur, proponam, quibus intellectis sapiens sapiencior erit." *Ibid.,* 175. This prologue is very suggestive of that of the Knight of La Tour Landry; see below, p. 134.

[82] *Ibid.,* 127–41.

[83] Crane says that Odo " left a collection of moralized fables and parables most industriously copied by later writers in this field. The value of Odo's work consists in the large number of fables which it aided most powerfully to diffuse through later collectors and preachers." *Jacques de Vitry,* introd., lxxxi. His influence on monkish legends should not be overlooked.

from the appearance of exempla not only in the sermons, of which Odo's collection stands as a model, but in didactic treatises like the *Gemma Ecclesiastica,* natural histories like the *De Naturis Rerum,* and works of information and correction, such as those of John of Salisbury, Walter Map, and Gervase of Tilbury. Still further, a range of sources, a variety of types, and a wealth of tales unknown to the pre-conquest period, have come into use. This comparative richness is to be explained by the acquaintance with Eastern material through the Crusades, the rise of the monastic orders, and the closer intercourse between English and Continental clerics and scholars, which promoted the circulation of the growing mass of anecdotes, fables, and legendary incidents.[84]

As to the number of special collections of Latin exempla which were made during the late twelfth and early thirteenth century, it is impossible to determine. Wright, in his edition of one hundred and forty-nine Latin stories selected from various collections of tales and fables,[85] states that "No manuscripts are of more frequent occurrence than collections of tales like those printed in the present volume."[86] A little later he says, "I am inclined to think that the period at which these collections began to be made was the earlier part of the thirteenth century, and that to that century we owe the compilation in Latin of most of these tales, though the greater number of manuscripts may be ascribed to the fourteenth."[87] From the prominence of the type already noted, it seems safe to assume that collections were begun even before the end of the twelfth century. The church libraries at that period were in possession of the classic example-books,[88] and that they were being used is suggested by an entry in the twelfth century catalogue

[84] The material for exempla, furnished by the Latin historians of the twelfth century, was considerable.

[85] The fables, Wright has taken largely from Odo de Ceritona's collection.

[86] *Latin Stories,* preface, vi.

[87] *Ibid.,* preface, vii.

[88] Among the books in the library at Lincoln Cathedral in 1150 were the "*Dialogum Gregorii*" and the "*Vitas Patrum*"; during the lifetime of the same custodian was added a "*Libellum de Vita Patrum.*" See *Giraldi Cambrensis Opera,* VII, Appendix C, 165 seq.

of the books at Durham, "Hi sunt libri qui leguntur Colla-
tionem." Under this heading are listed the following books:
*Vitae Patrum; Diadema Monachorum; Effrem cum Vitis
Egiptiorum; Paradisus; Speculum; Dialogus; Pastoralis, Exi-
mius Liber; Ysidorus de Summo Bono; Prosper de Contem-
plativa Vita; Liber Odonis; Johannes Cassianus; Decem Col-
lationes.*[89] The titles to be particularly noted are the *Vitae
Patrum,* the *Dialogus,* probably Gregory's *Dialogues,* and the
Lives of the Egyptians; others, such as the *Speculum* and the
Diadema Monachorum, are suggestive of exempla. Moreover,
the attention claimed by moral and religious anecdotes in the
twelfth century is amply evinced by the numerous compilations of saints' lives and legends of the Virgin,[90] which were
then produced. In the catalogues of the Lincoln and Durham
Cathedrals, the lives of saints are, next to Biblical exegesis,
the most numerous items. In Ward's *Catalogue,*[91] a discussion of the eleventh and twelfth century manuscripts of the
Miracles of the Virgin,[92] alone, occupies forty-seven pages.
Far more numerous were the collections of saints' lives. Considering these two classes of material, the mass of historical
and legendary incidents brought together by the Latin historians, the fable literature, the large amount of oral, traditional anecdote circulating among the clerics, and the exempla
already employed in treatises or compiled in small collections,
it is clear that the Latin writers of the twelfth century contributed much and gave a great impulse to the exemplum in
England before Jacques de Vitry and the friars ushered in its
flourishing period.

We may now consider the formal, Latin example-books

[89] *Catalogi Veteres Librorum Ecclesiae Cathedralis Dunelm,* 9.

[90] These legendary lives of holy men and women and the Virgin furnished
more exempla than any other class of material. In a sense, a saint's life
or a collection of saints' lives constituted a sort of example-book.

[91] H. L. D. Ward, *Catalogue of the Romances in the Department of
Manuscripts of the British Museum,* II, 595–642.

[92] For a thorough study of these, see Adolfo Mussafia, *Studien zu den
mittelälterlichen Marienlegenden,* in *Sitzungsberichte (Philosophisch-His-
torische Classe),* Band CXIX, Heft 2, s. 917; Band CXV, Heft I, s. 5;
Band CXIX, abh. 9; Band CXXIII, abh. 8.

which were produced in England after the middle of the thirteenth century. During the thirteenth and fourteenth centuries, example-books in England, as elsewhere, appear to be practically confined to Latin. France, Germany, and Italy were much more prolific than England in turning out exempla, although the clerics in the latter country were by no means idle. Manuscripts of monkish legends were produced copiously enough, but they were eclipsed by the more compendious and superior compilations of the Continent, such as the exempla from the sermons of Jacques de Vitry, the *Alphabetum Narrationum*, the *Tractatus* of Étienne de Bourbon, the *Directorium Vitae Humanae* of John of Capua, the *Speculum Historiale* of Vincent de Beauvais (?), and the *Dialogus Miraculorum* of Caesar of Heisterbach. Still, a few compilations were made on English ground, which have not fallen into oblivion; some of them are, indeed, among the most noted of their kind.

Until the close of the thirteenth century, apparently no famous collection was produced in England, but the time was preparing for a great work,—the *Gesta Romanorum*. We have, for example, a *Liber Exemplorum ad usum Praedicantium*,[93] compiled between 1270–79 by a Franciscan, probably of Warwickshire.[94] This book is a preachers' manual in two parts; the first part relates tales "De Rebus Superioribus," such as Christ, the Virgin, the angels, and St. James, arranged in order of importance; the second part narrates incidents "De Rebus Inferioribus," arranged alphabetically. There are two hundred and thirteen titles, and the list of sources, compiled by Little, comprises forty-three authors. The *Vitae Patrum*, from which the writer takes thirty-six exempla, is most prominent; then come in order of importance, the *Dialogues* of Gregory, the *Summa virtutum et vitiorum* of Paraldus, and the *Life of John of Alexandria;* less frequently

[93] Edited by A. C. Little for the Society of Franciscan Studies. The prologue is missing from the unique MS., B. IV. 19, Durham Cathedral, and the collection is preserved only to the letter M.

[94] The editor, from references in the exempla, concludes that the writer was a student in Paris about 1264–5, and that he later held clerical office in England. *Liber Exemplorum*, introd., vi seq.

quoted sources are the *Bible,* the classic theologians, such as Augustine, Gregory, and Beda, saints' lives, *Barlaam and Josaphat,* and historical compends, such as those of Peter Comestor and Beda.

Of particular significance are references in the work to other collections, now missing[95] but, judging from the tales cited, of about the same kind as that under discussion. One of these called *"Exempla Deodati"* furnished the *Liber Exemplorum* three tales. The first of these entitled " Quaedam mulier coniugata " tells of a woman of evil character who was incited by the devil " in specie iuvenis " to corrupt holy persons; she was saved by her son's penitence.[96] Another from this source narrates a conversation between a demon and " frater Iordan, magister ordinis predicatorum."[97] The third tells of a certain young man who, " amans illicite," entered the chamber of his noble lady one night only to be greeted with the cry, " A A A ! fuge, demon." Frightened out of his wits, he fled with greater speed than dignity to a near-by hermitage where, after confession, he was relieved of the devil which had transformed him.[98] Another missing collection cited by the author of the *Liber Exemplorum* is the *"Exempla Communia"* from which he takes three, possibly four, tales.[99] These are of the same monkish character, dealing with churchmen, demons, and miraculous happenings. These lost collections indicate that example-books must have been far more numerous before time and the destructive zeal of the Reformation reduced the number of such " talis of rybawdy and vain lesyngis."

The compiler of the *Liber Exemplorum,* however, like many

[95] Little states that he was unable to find the *Exempla Deodati.* He did, however, find one other reference to the collection in Balliol Coll. MS. 228 where it is represented by one exemplum. The work is here attributed to " Frater de ordine minorum, Deodatus nomine, quondam minister Hybernie." See *Liber,* 141–2, note.

[96] *Liber,* 54.

[97] *Ibid.,* 91.

[98] *Liber,* 121. The tale closes with a reference to its use in the sermons of one " frater de Wycumbe "; see also ibid., 88, for another reference to the use of exempla in contemporary sermons.

[99] *Ibid.,* 5, 61, 95, 125. Three of these cite the *Exempla Communia.*

other clerics, appears to have considered the tales highly meri-
torious. His exempla are directed "to the utility and edifica-
tion of the people, announcing to them vices and virtues,
punishment and glory."[100] He aims throughout to make the
use of tales beneficial and wholesome. Now he directs a warning to preachers to avoid vile words;[101] again, after certain
particularly vicious tales, he cautions preachers to modify them
in recital to the people, since they may suggest crimes hitherto
unknown.[102] Another caution, which was probably observed
widely, relates to the exercise of discrimination in the use of
tales dealing with sinning clerics.[103] These were to be employed when churchmen were addressed, but were not expedi-
tious for general use.[104] Not only did he aim to make the
exemplum a wholesome and worthy part of sermons, but he
also tried to make the tales of his collection stimulating by
using specific names, either as actors or personal narrators,

[100] *Liber,* introd., xiii.

[101] *Ibid.,* 98. " Caveat qui predicat ut verba curialia dicat, ut videlicet
nominet *lutum* pro *stercore, rem parvi valoris* pro *vili spermate."* See also
ibid., 200.

[102] *Ibid.,* 56, 115–16, 120–21.

[103] The monks did not seem to mind the disparaging tales about themselves, and they certainly took delight in those which dealt with the
secular clergy.

[104] *Liber,* 94–95. After narrating a tale of a wicked cleric who saw a
vision of hell awaiting him, the author says, " nec expedit de religiosis talia
populo pronunciare. . . . Si autem predicatur religiosis, tota narracia . . .
utilis erit." See also the tale preceding this. It is to be noted that although
the writer is a Franciscan he does not attempt in the tales to extol his
own order nor to cast reflections upon other orders. This is generally
true with reference to the thousands of stories told and retold by men of
the various monkish orders, Franciscans, Dominicans, Cistercians, Augus-
tinians, and others. The religious *dramatis personae* good and bad in the
narratives, are, as if by general understanding, of a universal class ; the
appellations, " a certain monk," " a pious hermit," " a wicked friar," etc.,
are pretty consistently adhered to. In some cases, to be sure, specific
names are mentioned, but they are commonly those of well-known men and
are by no means restricted to any particular order. In the present collection, for instance, the Franciscan collector speaks highly of several Dominicans, such as " Richard Fishacre of good memory " (p. 19), " Robertus
de Sudeseye, brother holy and noble " (p. 63) ; see also pp. 109, 123.

and specific places, particularly local ones.[105] The *Liber Exemplorum* is an energetic little book which points to considerable activity in England in the field of illustrative tales.

Similar to the *Liber Exemplorum* are other example-books which were compiled in England during the thirteenth century. Toward the end of the century appeared a large collection, alphabetically arranged under subject headings, and known as the *Speculum Laicorum*.[106] It has been attributed to John Hoveden, who died in 1275, but though it is undoubtedly the work of an Englishman, the evidence for Hoveden's authorship is very scanty.[107] The tales are arranged under ninety-one headings, beginning with "Abstinentia" and ending with "Usura"; they number five hundred and seventy-two. These include, besides the usual monkish legends, many delightful contemporary anecdotes[108] which help to account for the popularity of the work, indicated by the number of copies still preserved in the British Museum and the Bodleian.

In addition to such larger collections as those mentioned in the foregoing pages, and the Continental collections which were circulating among the clergy, smaller compilations abounded.[109] All these had been preparing the way for a work of exemplar literature in many respects unparalleled,—the *Gesta Roma-*

[105] Among writers of exempla there appears to have been little hesitation about joining a nine hundred year old event with a ninety year old name.

[106] The original MS., 11,284, Brit. Mus., is entitled "*Fabularum anecdotorumque collectio ad usum praedicantium, in seriem alphabeticam digestam.*" See Crane, *J. de V.*, introd., lxxii. Excerpts from the *Speculum* are printed in Haupt and Hoffman's *Altdeutsche Blätter*, Leipzig, 1840, II, 74–82. These are reprinted by Wright in *Latin Stories*.

[107] See J. A. Herbert, "The Authorship of the '*Alphabetum Narrationum*,'" in *Library*, January, 1905, p. 96.

[108] See *ibid.*, p. 96; also Crane, *J. de V.*, introd., lxxii. Contemporary with the *Speculum*, there appeared on the Continent two collections. One of these, containing about two hundred tales, was called the *Tractatus exemplorum de abundantia adaptorum ad omnem materiam in sermonibus, secundum ordinem alphabeti;* the other was the famous *Alphabetum Narrationum* of which a fifteenth century English translation is preserved. The latter, *An Alphabet of Tales,* has been edited by Mrs. Mary M. Banks for the E. E. T. S.

[109] See Crane, *J. de V.*, introd., lxxii–lxxiii.

norum.[110] Concerning this book which is so well-known and
has been the subject of so much scholarly investigation, little
need be said here.[111] The few facts which concern us particularly may be briefly stated. The *Gesta* was, in its original form,
a collection of Latin narratives drawn from oriental apologues,
monkish legends, classical stories, tales of the chroniclers,
popular traditions, and furnished with apposite moralizations
after the manner of Odo de Ceritona's moralized fables and
the *Contes Moralizés* of Nicole de Bozon. "Its object was
undoubtedly," says Herrtage, "to furnish a series of entertaining tales to the preachers of the day or to monastic societies,
accompanied by such allegorical forms of exposition as to con-
vey, according to the taste of the age, information of a theological character or moral tendency."[112] The collection appeared at the end of the thirteenth or the opening of the fourteenth century.[113] Oesterley repudiates the ascriptions to the
most favored claimant, Pierre Bercheur, and concludes that it
is impossible to determine the compiler. Considering the
absence of substantial evidence, it is no wonder for, as the
learned editor asks, "Who during the thirteenth and fourteenth centuries, did not tell parables and tales in the style
of the *Gesta,* who did not moralize, and what was not moralized?"[114] The most significant fact in connection with the
present discussion is that all indications point to England as the
place of compilation.[115] This circumstance undoubtedly gave
a special prominence to exampla in England, but it must be
realized that for the most part the *Gesta* is no more English

[110] The following are the best editions: Sir Frederick Madden, Middle
English text, for the Roxburghe Club, 1838; Herman Oesterley, Latin text,
Berlin, 1872; S. J. H. Herrtage, Middle English text, for the E. E. T. S.,
No. 33; Rev. Chas. Swan, Modern English, New York, 1905.

[111] From the time of Warton and Douce, the *Gesta* has been the subject of painstaking research. Since Oesterley's masterly work was published in 1872, nothing material has been added.

[112] *Gesta,* ed. Herrtage, introd., viii. The popularity and influence of the
work is suggested by the fact that no less than one hundred and sixty-six
manuscripts have been found. *Ibid.,* xxvii.

[113] *Gesta,* ed. Oesterley, 257.

[114] *Ibid.,* 254–55.

[115] *Ibid.,* 262.

than French, German, or Italian. It represents the universal clerical spirit of an age in which story-telling had a sort of practical value.

It would, of course, be an error to consider this great collection merely an example-book. The early date, the Latin language, and the general tone of the work indicate that it was designed primarily for clerics;[116] but it is more than a preachers' manual. Mingled with many fables and short, typical exempla,[117] are a greater number of elaborated and purely secular tales.[118] It may, therefore, with some propriety be looked upon as a transitional work between collections of exempla and compilations of tales which, though sometimes didactic in tone, were largely secular in content, were more pleasingly told for popular entertainment, and left the lesson to be drawn without the aid of an explanation. On the one side the *Gesta* points to the collections of Gregory, Nicole de Bozon, and Jacques de Vitry; on the other, to the stories of Boccaccio, Gower, and Chaucer.[119]

After the appearance of the *Gesta,* there is a notable increase in the number of secular tales in exempla-books. Often the place of the more obvious moral of the monkish legend is sup-

[116] The tales are unclassified, but, as was noted in the introductory chapter, the combination of tabulation and moralization was not introduced, apparently, until Johannes Junior's *Scala Celi,* about 1350.

[117] The following representative titles need no explanation: how a clerk was saved by confession and penance from a compact with the devil (Herrtage, p. 375); how a nail dropped into the balance of good-deeds when a good and a bad angel stood disputing over a departing soul (p. 379); how a man was delivered for his piety (p. 379); how certain tempting devils were vanquished (p. 380); how a bishop was damned for neglecting God's warning (p. 380); how a rich man was punished for robbing a poor widow (p. 386); old favorites, such as the man chased by a unicorn, the rustic who drank ditch-water, and the test for the true son, are not wanting.

[118] Typical of this group are: the story of Lear and his three daughters, the three caskets, the pound of flesh, the tale of Constance, the race of Atalanta, Androclus and the lion, Vergil's speaking statue.

[119] D'Ancona assumes the influence of monkish on secular collections, the beginning of which he puts at the opening of the fourteenth century. See *Studi di Critica e storia letteraria,* 252. Garnett says that *Il Novellino* was compiled about the middle of the thirteenth century "with a distinct moral purpose." *A History of Italian Literature,* 85.

plied by the attachment of an ingenious moralization. The next important collections compiled in England illustrate this new departure. These were two books by an English Dominican, John Holkot, who was a professor of theology at Oxford at the time of his death in 1349.[120] One of these works, the *Liber de Moralizationibus*,[121] consists largely of classical stories from Ovid, Pliny, Valerius Maximus, and ancient history. Each story is provided with an elaborate moralization called an "expositio moralis," or "tropologia." The collection, although the manuscripts contain only from forty-seven to seventy-five tales,[122] had considerable popularity. It stands with the same writer's *Liber Sapientiae* as the most notable example-book compiled in England between the *Gesta Romanorum* and Bromyard's *Summa Praedicantium*.

Holkot's *Liber Sapientiae*[123] consists of nineteen chapters subdivided into two hundred and eleven "lectiones." The "lectiones," which run together in a very confusing manner, treat a great number of topics which occupied the attention of contemporary clerics, such as adultery, avarice, and other sins, the love of God, reward of virtue, punishment of evil, miracles, and scores of allied subjects.[124] These discussions are guided by Biblical texts freely interspersed, and are illustrated by a heterogeneous mass of historical and classical learning, figures of speech, natural history passages, and exempla comprising fables, monkish legends, and secular tales.[125] Despite an index, the material is not conveniently tabulated but it appears to have been very popular among the

[120] See *Dictionary of National Biography*.

[121] The work is otherwise known as *Liber de Moralitatibus*, or simply *Moralitates*. It is printed with the *Liber Sapientiae*, Basel, 1586.

[122] See Oesterley's *Gesta*, 246. Some of Holkot's tales are drawn from the *Gesta*.

[123] It is sometimes called *Opus super Sapientiam Solomonis*.

[124] The book may be compared in general method of composition to Burton's *Anatomy of Melancholy*, although the relative clearness of topical division in the latter is marked. A prefixed "tabula," corresponding rudely to our index, furnishes an aid to those sufficiently initiated to use it.

[125] As Crane has pointed out, the extraordinary number of citations from pagan authorities is noteworthy. *J. de V.*, introd., xcix.

learned, for no less than eight editions were called for before 1500.[126]

But Holkot's works, and even the *Gesta*, are surpassed as collections of exempla by the last great Latin example-book compiled in England, John Bromyard's *Summa Praedicantium*,[127] a gigantic work which rivals the most famous Continental collections. Like Holkot, Bromyard was a Dominican. He was educated at Oxford and became distinguished in jurisprudence there, as well as at Cambridge, where he lectured on theology; his work was, therefore, exceptionally influential. The great *Summa* contains more than a thousand exempla; as Goedke remarks, "Scarcely any other work is so rich in fables and tales."[128]

The book is divided into one hundred and eighty-nine chapters, treating as many topics arranged alphabetically, as, "gaudium," "gloria," "gratia," "gratitudo," "gula," etc. Mingled with the discussion on these topics are the exempla, usually indicated by the word "exemplum" in the margin. As Crane puts it, they represent "the whole body of mediaeval and classical literature known to the learned. Scarcely any department of these two great divisions is unrepresented: fables, legends, mediaeval epics, Oriental apologues, anecdotes from Roman history, from Biblical history, popular jests, etc."[129] It included most of the choice tales from all former collections of the kind.[130] With its completion at the opening of the fifteenth century,[131] the Latin example-book reached its highest development, not only for England but for the world.

[126] See Hain, *Repertorium Bibliographicum.*

[127] First edition without place or date (probably Basel, 1485), 2 vols., folio (Union Theological Seminary). Other editions are: Nuremberg, 1485, 1518, 1578; Paris, 1518; Lyons, 1522; Venice, 1586; Antwerp, 1614 (Yale).

[128] See *Orient und Occident,* I, 538.

[129] See " *Mediaeval Sermon-books and Stories,*" in *Proceedings of the Amer. Philosophical Society* for 1883, XXI, 71.

[130] The present treatment of the *Summa* is frankly disproportionate to the size of this enormous monument to the collector's industry. But the work may be said to differ from those already treated, in bulk rather than in kind.

[131] Bromyard died in 1418. See *D. N. B.;* also Crane, " *Mediaeval Sermon-books and Stories,*" *Amer. Phil. Soc.,* XXI, 70.

To sum up,—England was largely indebted to Continental sources for the tales in her formal example-books, and in the number of famous collections was not so fruitful as Germany, France, and Italy, where churchmen were more numerous and tales had a greater circulation. But, aside from smaller compilations, her contribution was by no means insignificant, as is shown by the *Liber Exemplorum,* the *Speculum Laicorum,* the *Gesta Romanorum,* the *Liber de Moralizationibus,* the *Liber Sapientiae,* and the *Summa Praedicantium.*

CHAPTER IV

The Exemplum in Popular Homiletic Literature after the Coming of the Friars

At the opening of the thirteenth century, as we have seen, exempla were chiefly confined to Latin literature and were in the hands of clerics and scholars; larger use in the vernacular was needed to bring them into more common knowledge. This end was advanced mainly by the coming of the Dominican and Franciscan friars, who completely revolutionized preaching in England, as elsewhere. It has already been shown that at the opening of the thirteenth century there was little preaching; and that this was practically confined to the country districts. "In the towns there were but few priests, and these were frequently but ill-educated and unfitted to cope with the difficulties of the situation."[1] J. S. Brewer, in the preface to the *Monumenta Franciscana,* says, "The inhabitant of the town . . . had to struggle on to light and order, self-taught and self-sustained."[2] The change which resulted with the coming of the friars was immediate, and their success pronounced.[3] The Dominicans came to Dover early in August, 1221, and were cordially received by Archbishop Langton. On August 10, they were preaching in London, and on the 15th they appeared in Oxford. Just three years later, on September 11, 1224, came the Franciscans, who quickly spread throughout the populous districts. By the autumn of 1225 they were established at Canterbury and London; in 1226 they were settled in Lynn, Yarmouth, and Norwich. Welcomed and encouraged by Grosseteste, Bishop of Lincoln,[4] they were soon working in other towns, such as York, Bristol, and Shrewsbury. Some of England's best men joined the order; others came

[1] Father Cuthbert, *The Friars and how they came to England,* 4.
[2] *Monumenta Franciscana,* I, preface, xi.
[3] A. Jessop, *The Coming of the Friars,* 32–33.
[4] See F. S. Stevenson, *Robert Grosseteste,* 32, 59 seq., 146.

84

from abroad. Thirty years after their first arrival, there were in England twelve hundred and forty-two Franciscans, with forty-nine monasteries.[5] Surely England had experienced an awakening. Bishop Grosseteste, in a letter to Pope Gregory IX, writes, about 1238: "They [the friars] illuminate the whole country with the light of their preaching and learning. ... If your Holiness could see with what devotion and humility the people run to hear the word of life from them, for confession and instruction in daily life, and how much improvement the clergy and the regulars have obtained *by imitating them,*[6] you would indeed say that 'upon them that dwell in the light of the shadow of death hath the light shined.' "[7] A new religious era in England had begun.

The wonderful success of the friars was due in great part to their homiletic method. Previous to their coming, the clergy had become incapable of making an effective appeal, because of their addiction to law and logic. Giraldus Cambrensis complains of this tendency and attributes to such scholastic pursuits the inefficiency of his contemporaries in the pulpit.[8] This dry scholasticism had been somewhat mitigated by 1200, owing to the establishment of Peter Lombard's *Sentences* as a standard text-book in the theological schools. The work constituted, in a measure, a reaction against the excessive use of abstract reasoning in sermons. Aiming to substitute authority for logic, Peter Lombard's plan was to collect under the heads of important theological questions, such statements from Scripture and patristic writings as aided in the solution thereof.[9] But a more practical and appealing method was

[5] Jessop, *op. cit.,* 34 seq.

[6] The italics are mine.

[7] Stevenson, *op. cit.,* 79.

[8] *Giraldi Cambrensis Opera,* II, Chap. xxxvii, "*De literaturae defectu ex legum humanarum et logices abusu proveniente*"; see also *Mon. Fran.,* preface, xxxiv, lxxxvii.

[9] Stevenson, *op. cit.,* 19. It is to be noted that Peter Lombard simply brought into compact form, a class of material which had always been more or less favored; he systematized the appeal to authorities. His work may be said to have become the starting-point for an entirely new set of commentaries.

instituted by these friars, who went out " to preach the gospel to all the world." Preaching, which had been occupied with abstract discussions and formal statements of doctrine, became human, simple, and personal.[10] The friars told of Christ's life at Nazareth, of his pity, love and compassion. Their message was spoken from wide experience and in plain, unaffected language. Incidents of daily life, drawn from constant intercourse with all sorts and conditions of men, were freely used for illustrations.[11] " Their sermons," says Brewer, " are full of pithy stories and racy anecdotes; now introducing some popular tradition or legend, now enforcing a moral by some fable or allegory."[12] The stories which had been accumulating in the cloisters, reposing in Latin collections and treatises, and at most only scantily represented in the pulpit, were now poured out in the vernacular by the enthusiastic friars who overran Europe.[13]

[10] *Mon. Fran.*, preface, xxxviii.

[11] *The Friars and how they came to England,* 106–7. The Franciscans, and particularly the Dominicans, conveyed much dogmatic instruction on the chief truths of religion, but they made these truths alive and appealing. It is of interest to observe in the contemporary mystery and morality plays, the same desire to vitalize and visualize religious and moral teaching.

[12] *Mon. Fran.*, preface, li.

[13] Lecoy de la Marche says: Il ne faut pas oublier que les deux nouveaux ordres voués au ministère de la parole, les Frères Prêcheurs et les Frères Mineurs, s'en allant à travers les villes et villages, haranguant les fidèles sur les places publiques aussi bien que dans l'Église, sur les grands chemins comme dans les lieux consacrés, avaient le plus souvent affaire à des auditoires simples et naïfs. L'éloquence populaire était leur fait; ils récitaient point des discours savants; ils n'entraient guère dans les raisonnements ni dans les abstractions. Ils improvisaient, ils instruisaient, et ils racontaient." *Anecdotes historiques,* introd., 11. Meray, after speaking of the widespread influence of the Dominicans and Franciscans, says: " Il [the friar] ne négligea rien pour intéresser son auditoire: fables ingenieuses, pantomimes bizarres, contes grivois, légendes dramatisées. Leurs sermons étaient pour le peuple un répertoire inepuisable d'émotions tour à tour comiques et tragiques du plus vivant effet." *La Vie au Temps des libres Prêcheurs,* I, 55–6. See also *Deutsche Predigten der XIII und XIV Jahrhunderten (Bibl. der gesammt. deutsch. nat. Lit.)*, edited by Dr. Herman Leyser, introd., 15; also W. Scherer, *A History of German Literature,* translated by Mrs. F. C. Conybeare, I, 226–27.

The popular sermons of these friars during the first half of the thirteenth century are rarely preserved. The fact seems to be that a large amount of this preaching was extempore and with the Franciscans remained so for a long time.[14] After the middle of the century, Dominican collections of Latin sermons containing exempla become more plentiful. They were commonly designed for the Sunday and Festival services of the whole year, and were often supplied with an appended collection of exempla, known as a *promptuarium*. Among the notable works of this kind, England is not represented until the time of John Felton, who flourished about 1430.[15] But although such monuments are wanting, the exemplum, as we have seen, had been popularized by the friars.

Except in the sermons, which were still written in Latin, the exemplum was rarely used during the thirteenth century.[16] Here and there a few scattered instances may be found. *Vices and Virtues,* for example, written about 1200, contains several Biblical references and one developed exemplum.[17] The *Ancren Riwle,* influenced probably by Aldhelm's *De Laudibus Virginitatis* and other Latin treatises, also contains a few. In speaking of the *Ancren Riwle,* Ten Brink says, "We cannot fail to recognize the workings of a new school of

[14] Aubertin says: " L'éloquence des Frères mineurs ou Franciscains était plus simple et plus familière que celle des Dominicains; alors même qu'ils subirent l'empire de la scholastique, leur prédication garda une allure toute populaire. C'est ce qui nous explique le petit nombre de leurs sermons écrits." *Histoire de la Langue et de la Littérature françaises,* II, 316.

[15] See *D. N. B.;* also Crane, *J. de V.,* introd., lxi–lxii. In this introduction Crane gives (pp. liii seq.) a very satisfactory account of the notable collections of the kind under discussion. They proceeded largely from the Dominicans of France, Italy, and especially Germany.

[16] It is very likely that many works containing exempla have been destroyed. Small, in the introduction to the *English Metrical Homilies,* says : " This collection is remarkable in many respects, more especially from its containing numerous legends of saints and illustrative tales, which must have rendered it a very popular book in the Middle Ages. At the same time these legends in all probability marked it out as an object of mutilation or destruction at the period of the Reformation, when so many memorials of the former religion were destroyed by the zeal of the reformers."

[17] *V. and V.,* Pt. I, 148. The exemplum is from the *Vitae Patrum.*

preachers, though the author neither resorts to the most common topics of daily life nor interweaves any true fables [eigentliche Märchen] into his work."[18] This is not quite true, since one of the indications of this new school, which Ten Brink has perhaps overlooked, is the presence of narrative illustrations. A number of these are brief references. For instance, the evil of too much "looking" is exemplified by Lucifer's fatal self-admiration; likewise, Eve became sinful by seeing the apple which wrought such destruction.[19] Monkish legends, however, are not wanting. Four of these are narrated in some detail and four others appear as familiar references. To illustrate the efficacy of prayer, the writer tells the oft-repeated legend of the flying fiend who was stopped by a holy man at prayer.[20] He then adds, as if the incident needed only recalling, "Have ye not heard also this of the devil Ruffinus, Belial's brother, in our English book of St. Margaret?[21] And the other devil of which we read that he cried loudly to St. Bartholomew, who was much in prayer, and said: 'Incendunt me orationes tuae.'" In speaking of the necessity of keeping ever upright, he tells of a woman who in an unguarded moment was beguiled by the devil and continued in sin for twenty years.[22] To show the evil consequences of incomplete confession, the much-favored return-from-death theme is used.[23] References to "another man" and "a lady," who had well nigh been damned for trivial faults, follow the above tale. In cautioning the anchoresses against all carnal ease and indulgence, he asks, "And have ye never heard the story of the three holy men?" One of these was wont to use hot spices and to lust after meat and drink, whereas the other two, even when sick, took what God sent them "nor ever made much ado about ginger, or valerian, or cloves." One day the

---

[18] *History of English Literature*, I, 201.

[19] *Ancren Riwle*, 53; for similar illustrations see pp. 55, 57, 67, 122, 155, 161, 171, 271, 299, 335.

[20] *Ibid.*, 245.

[21] The Lives of St. Margaret, St. Juliana, and St. Katherine had recently appeared in English.

[22] *Ancren Riwle*, 267.

[23] *Ibid.*, 315.

three fell asleep and the Queen of Heaven came with two hand-maidens who bore a spoon of gold and an electuary. The Queen directed the maidens to attend two of the men but not the eater of spices, for, as she said, "'He is his own physician.'"[24] Before drawing the moral, the writer says, "A holy man stood not far off and beheld all this."[25] These exempla are told in good faith by the learned author, but instead of being drawn from his own experience they are taken from the saints' legends or other collections of pious tales, which were now becoming plentiful throughout the Christian world. The implication that the women probably knew some of these incidents is suggestive of some familiarity with the legends, at least among the elect.

But while, during the thirteenth century, the exemplum was being popularized in the pulpit, it was, apparently, little used elsewhere. A long time elapses after the *Ancren Riwle* (c. 1225) before we reach another English work employing exempla. Then, greatly influenced and increased in number by saints' legends, the type appears in greater prominence than ever before.

In view of the importance of saints' legends, not only as material for exempla but as substitutes for sermons, we may turn for a moment to English hagiography.[26] From the very

[24] *Ancren Riwle,* 371.

[25] An amusing note on the margin of the manuscript runs, "'David Frys, of Brantom, may believe this storie, whoe hath al read it.'"

[26] Although they constitute a prolific source for exempla, the Latin lives of individual saints, produced in such great numbers both in England and on the Continent, and the voluminous Latin collections, such as the *Vitae Patrum* and the *Acta Sanctorum,* may only be mentioned here. As Scherer says, there is, even in the eleventh century, an "enormous wealth of sacred legends, forming a complete Christian heroic cycle, and running through the whole scale from harmless pious tales to exciting sensational romances." *A History of German Literature,* I, 74. See Horstmann, *Altenglische Legenden,* Neue Folge, introd., for a brief but good study of the legendaries. Among the Latin lives produced in England may be mentioned Aelfric's *Vita Aethelwoldi,* Lanferth's *Miracula S. Swithini,* Eadmer's *Vita Anselmi,* Wm. of Malmesbury's *Vita Aldhelmi.* Then, under Norman influence, came the saints' legends of such men as Wace, Walter Map, John of Salisbury, and Gervase of Tilbury. See Horstmann, *Altengl. Leg.,* N. F., introd., xli–xlii.

beginnings of English literature, the lives of saints were popular. In the second half of the eighth century we have the *Guthlac, Juliana, Andreas,* and *Elene*,[27] and after the reformation directed by Dunstan and Aethelwold there was increased zeal in the production of saints' lives. The chief result was Aelfric's *Metrical Lives of Saints* (996–97), translated from Latin originals.[28] In his greeting to Aethelwerd, Aelfric refers to the former homilies which contained "passions and lives of the saints which the English nation honoreth with festivals." "Now," he continues, "it has seemed good to us that we should write this book concerning the sufferings and lives of the saints whom monks in their offices honor amongst themselves."[29] In Skeat's edition there are thirty-seven chapters, which, with a few exceptions (de Temporale), were intended to be read as homilies for the Saints' Days ordained by the Church.[30] Bruno Assman has printed other Old English saints' lives: two of St. Margaret, the legend of the holy Veronica, and three lives from the *Vitae Patrum*, all of which are in prose.[31]

Then came the beginning of the universal flourishing period of the legend,[32] with the three early Middle English lives of

[27] All were based on Latin originals. See Körting, *Grundriss* (1905 ed.), 53–6. A poem on Thomas, similar to the *Andreas*, must have existed, for Aelfric states, "The passion of Thomas we leave unwritten because it has long since been turned into English in song-wise." *Homilies*, II, 521.

[28] Aelfric says of them, "transtulimus de Latinitate ad usitatam Anglicam sermocinationem." *Lives of Saints*, I, 2. On the sources see the dissertation by J. H. Ott, *Über die Quellen der Heiligenleben in Aelfric's Lives of Saints.* According to Ott, the chief sources were: Mombritius, *Sanctuarium sive Vitae Sanctorum;* Surius, *De probatis sanctorum historiis;* and the *Acta Sanctorum.* Many other works, such as the *Vitae Patrum*, the writings of Gregory the Great, and Beda's *Ecclesiastical History*, were used.

[29] Aelfric's *Lives of Saints*, I, 5.

[30] Cf. the *Menologium, or Saints' Calendar*, published in Grein-Wülker's *Bibl. der angels. Poesie*, II, 282 seq. On the legendaries and other reading-books of the Church, see Wordsworth and Littlehales, *The Old Service-Books of the English Church*, 129 seq.

[31] *Angelsächsische Homilien und Heiligenleben*, printed in Grein-Wülker's *Bibl. der angels. Prosa*, III, 170 seq.

[32] "Um 1200 begann sich dieselbe geistliche Minne in der umfangreicheren Gattung zu äussern. Die lateinische Legende war im Laufe des XII.

St. Margaret,[33] *St. Juliana,* and *St. Katherine,* based upon Latin originals, which are abridged or elaborated with a freedom characteristic of English legend translators and compilers.[34]   These pieces were calculated to inspire in women emulation of the saintly life which was receiving such encouragement at the opening of the thirteenth century.   It was at about this time that the Anglo-Norman, Chardri, produced his marvelous legend, the *Sept Dormants;* and in 1212 appeared in England a verse translation of Gregory's *Dialogues,* containing many abstracts from saints' lives.[35]

Between 1270–90 appeared on the Continent a collection of Latin saints' legends which, owing to its complete and well-written list of lives, soon superseded the scattered legends as a source of exempla.[36]   This was the famous *Legenda Aurea*[37] of Jacobus de Voragine, Archbishop of Genoa.   It formed the

Jahrhunderts unter Aufnahme keltischer und orientalischer Heiliger so aufgeblüht, dass sie die Geschichtschreibung überwucherte, besonders bei William von Malmesbury, Henry von Huntington, Geoffrey von Monmouth, also in der Nachbarschaft des bardenreichen Wales." Brandl, in Paul's *Grundriss,* II, Pt. I, 617.

[33] The editor, Oswald Cockayne, prints a prose version which he calls " a text of 1200," and a poetic version which he calls " a text of 1330."

[34] See *Life of St. Katherine,* introd., xx.   Horstmann says of the pieces under discussion, " Sie stehen offenbar unter der Einwirkung des französischen Kunstepos, doch ist der Stil durchaus eigenartig national, echt volkstümlich episch, eher germanischen als französischen Characters, mit eigenthümlichen Wendungen, Attributen und Gleichnissen, plastisch, und von tiefster Empfindung durchdrungen." *Altengl. Leg.,* N. F., introd., xlii.

[35] See Gaston Paris, *La Littérature française au Moyen Age,* 232. Anglo-Normans, such as Wace, and many Frenchmen were actively engaged in turning out legends of the Virgin, saints' lives, and translations of the classic oriental collections of tales, such as the *Seven Sages,* and the *Barlaam and Josaphat,* during the thirteenth century.   See *ibid.,* Chap. V, " *Les Légendes hagiographiques.*"

[36] See Crane, *J. de V.,* introd., lxx.

[37] Dr. Graesse's edition of the *Legenda* contains no fewer than two hundred and forty-three items.   An English translation of the book was finished in 1438.   Another English version, made by Caxton from " a legend in French, another in Latin, and a third in English," was twice printed (1484 and 1487?).   Horstmann, *Altengl. Leg.,* N. F., introd., cxxx. It is worthy of note that an abridgment of the *Barlaam and Josaphat* was used in the *Legenda Aurea.*   See Ward's *Catalogue,* II, 129 seq.   Caxton's *Golden Legend* has been edited by F. S. Ellis, 7 vols., Temple Classics, 1900.

basis of such later English compilations as the legendary attributed to Barbour,[38] Mirk's *Festial* (c. 1400), and Bokenham's *Lives of Saints* (1443–46).[39]

Slightly later, probably, than the *Legenda Aurea,* was produced the notable collection of legends in English, known as the *South English Legendary,*[40] the work of the monks of the Abbey of Gloucester. The collection consists of narratives for each of the saints' days, and a "Temporale" for the festivals of Christ, the Advent, Christmas, the Passion, and Easter; in some manuscripts there is also a life of Christ.[41] Before it was completed, parts of it seem to have been circulated and augmented in neighboring abbeys, with the result that the numerous manuscripts differ considerably in details.[42] As might be expected from such a method of production, the work is uneven and sometimes crude; but the accounts of sacrifice, purity, compassion, holiness, and other virtues and vices, were sufficiently artistic to satisfy the preachers and moralists who used them as exempla.

Before passing to the *North English Legend and Homily Collection,* I wish to mention the *Cursor Mundi,* that ponderous narrative compilation from Biblical and secular sources, saints' legends, *contes dévots,* and apochryphal gospels. Like the works which we have been considering, the *Cursor Mundi* was an effort to put into permanent vernacular form the treasures which abounded in Latin. This attempt to stimulate religious observance and morality in the people by holding up to admiration the lives of Christ, Mary, and holy men, had already to a certain extent been made through the pulpit. Early in the history of the Church the legend played a part in

[38] The attribution has been seriously questioned; see *Camb. Hist. of Eng. Lit.,* II, 146.

[39] See Horstmann, *Altengl. Leg.,* N. F., introd., xxxix.

[40] *The Early South English Legendary,* edited by Horstmann. The editor states (Pt. I, introd., viii) that the *Legenda Aurea* and the *S. E. Legendary* were independently compiled.

[41] See *ibid.,* introd., xiii–xxiv, for contents of the MSS.

[42] As is usually the case with collections of this kind, the number of titles increases with the later manuscripts; the earliest (1285–95) has sixty-seven items; the latest (fifteenth century) has one hundred and thirty-five.

the service.   At first it appeared only as a minor interpolation
into such offices as the mass; later it came to have a prominent
place, and even supplanted the gospels in the festival services.[43]
A number of the *Blickling* and *Old English Homilies* are, as I
pointed out, narratives of the lives of holy men.   Aelfric's
Sermones contained several of the same kind, and his *Lives
of Saints* was a thoroughgoing effort, the first in English, to
supply a complete set of festival homilies.   The flourishing
period of the saints' legends found adequate expression in the
South English Legendary, and the *North English Collection,*[44]
which appeared shortly after.   So highly favored were the
legends at this time that where they had not wholly supplanted
the gospels, as in the Sunday sermons, they were almost as
prominent in the office of exempla,[45] which rivaled in length the
Biblical portions of the discourses.

[43] " Schon in der ältesten Zeit wurden an den Festtagen der Heiligen
besondere Sermones de sanctis gehalten, worin der Bischof oder Prediger
die vor der Epistel gelesene Legende besprach; später, zur Zeit der Herr-
schaft der Homilie, wurden eigene Homilien für die Heiligenfeste über den
Text des festtäglichen Evangeliums unter die Homiliensammlung aufge-
nommen."   Horstmann, *Altengl. Leg.,* N. F., introd., xxiv.

[44] It is of interest to observe the characteristic diversity of matter and
manner in the legend collections, with their subjects drawn, now from
the Orient, now from Ireland; at one time rising to the most delicate poetic
expression, and again dealing crudely with the most ludicrous or revolting topics.

[45] In addition to the collected legends, and the single lives previously
mentioned, there were now available for exempla many separate Middle
English legends dealing with such subjects as St. Eustace, St. Ethelred,
St. Edmund, and St. Christopher.   Printed by Horstmann, *Altengl. Leg.,*
N. F.   There were also numerous *contes dévots,* such as " *Marina* "
(Altengl. Leg., 1878 ed.) and legends of the Virgin.   For examples of
these, see Herrig's *Archiv,* LVI, where nine, the remains of a large collection, are printed from the Vernon MS.   Fifteen brief prose Mary
legends appear in *Anglia,* for 1880.   All the legends of this sort give
striking proof, in the words of a typical introduction, of

> " How owre lady helpe cane
>   That to hyre clepe at nede."

(" Of the good knight and his jealous wife "; see *Altengl. Leg.,* N. F., 329).
France was even more active in the production and translation (from the
Latin) of Mary legends.   The most notable collection was the *Miracles de*

This was the situation at the opening of the fourteenth century, when the friars had thoroughly established the exemplum, which now began to appear in large numbers in English sermons and didactic treatises. We may proceed to examine four important collections of popular homiletic literature, which represent the nature and prominence of exempla in fourteenth century sermons. The *North English Homily Collection* belongs to the early part of the century; the *Contes Moralizés* of Nicole de Bozon appeared about the end of the first quarter; the prose treatises of Richard Rolle and his followers close the mid-century; and John Mirk's *Festial* comes at the end.

The *North English Homily Collection*[46] is a set of verse homilies which, though probably intended for general distribution, was read in church, just as were the saints' lives.[47] There was still, apparently, a lack of gospel literature in the vernacular for the author in his prologue writes

> " On Ingelis tong that alle may
> Understand quat I wil say,
> For laued men havis mar mister,
> Godes word for to her,
> Than klerkes that thair mirour lokes,
> And sees hou thai sal lif on bokes,
> And bathe klerk and laued man,
> Englis understand kan,
> That was born in Ingeland,
> And lang haves ben thar in wonand,
> Bot al men can noht, I wis,

Nostre Dame of Gautier de Coinci (d. 1236), previously mentioned. See Gaston Paris, *op. cit.*, Chap. IV, *"La Légende de la Vierge."* For a more extended study, see Mussafia, *loc. cit.*, above, p. 74.

[46] *English Metrical Homilies*, edited by John Small. This edition of a part of the *N. E. Hom. Coll.* is based upon the fragmentary fourteenth century MS., Edinburgh, Royal College of Physicians. Besides this MS. there are seven others of the original form of the collection, one of which contains the exempla only. There are also four expanded and two fragments of expanded collections. All of these, except MS. Phillipps 8254 which he did not know, are minutely described by Horstmann, *Altengl. Leg.*, N. F. introd., lx seq.

[47] A direction following a Latin passage in one of the sermons runs, " Isti versus omittantur a lectore quando legit Anglicum coram laycis." *Eng. Metr. Hom.*, 28.

Understand Latin and Frankis,
Forthi me think almous it isse,
To wirke sum god thing on Inglisse."[48]

In general plan, these homilies are similar to the *Ormulum;* that is, they open with a paraphrase of Scriptural text and continue with an exposition which frequently follows the traditional method of symbolism. Citations from St. Augustine, Gregory, and Beda also recall the earlier school, but in flexibility and conciseness of style the collection shows plainly the effects of Norman influence. Moreover, a marked difference is to be noted in the use of an exemplum at the close of each homily.

The illustrative tale is here prominent. The homilist leads up to the chief lesson of the discourse and then illustrates or confirms the point by a narrative, usually as long as the preceding discussion. These exempla,[49] being in verse and considerably influenced by the legendaries, are more literary in character than the brusque example-book versions. The number of sources drawn upon is fairly large and the diversity of the tales correspondingly great. From Professor Gerould's admirable study of the tales,[50] I am able to make the following tabulation, which indicates the kind of tales and the sources used. I shall group according to sources, following Professor Gerould's numbering of the tales.

Vitae Patrum
6 St. Anthony and the snares
7 St. Machary
19 The uncharitable hermit
23 The hermit and the thieves
26 The devil in church
24 Taysis
37 The monk who was harsh in judging
41 The thrifty gardner[51]

[48] *Eng. Metr. Hom.,* 3–4.

[49] The most complete edition of the tales (forty-five) is that by Horstmann, printed from one of the expanded versions, in Herrig's *Archiv,* LVII, 241–316.

[50] *The North-English Homily Collection, a Study of the Manuscript Relations and the Sources of the Tales.* Gerould has given full synopses of the tales found in the eight manuscripts of the unexpanded collections.

[51] This story may have been taken from the *Speculum Morale,* or from the *Summa virtutum ac vitiorum* of Paraldus.

The Bible

1 Mary Magdalene
3 The death of John the Baptist
9 The three kings
12 Gehazi and Naaman
30 The mother and her sons
36 The story of creation
50 The story of Esther

Legenda Aurea

10 St. John and the boy
17 St. Bernard and the peasant
20 The knight beguiled by the devil
21 St. Bede and the birds
22 Piers the usurer
45 St. Gregory and Trajan's soul[52]
54 Simon Magus

Legends of the Virgin

2 The monk who returned from death
4 The pilgrim to St. James
51 The widow's candle
52 The prioress who was miraculously delivered

Anonymous Exempla Collections

28 Theobald and the leper
29 The monk who prayed to see the joys of heaven[53]
40 The adulterous priest[54]

Alphabetum Narrationum[55]

33 The obedient servant
48 The despised nun

Speculum Morale[56]

14 The devil as physician
24 The man in the devil's leash

[52] Possibly from the *Alphabetum Narrationum,* or from the *Summa* of Paraldus.

[53] Possibly from Nicole de Bozon's *Contes Moralizés.*

[54] Possibly from William of Wadington's *Manuel des Pechiez.*

[55] Until recently, the Dominican, Étienne de Bescançon (d. 1294), has been generally accepted as the compiler. The weakness of this attribution was exposed by Heaureau in *Not. et Extr.,* II, 68–75, and again called in question by J. A. Herbert in *Library,* Jan., 1905, 94–101. Mr. Herbert advocates the authorship of Arnold of Liège.

[56] Long attributed to Vincent de Beauvais but probably not his. See E. Boutaric, *Revue des Questions Historiques,* XVII, 5.

Homilies of Gregory

42 The wicked brother of a monk
47 Tarsilla, Gordiana and Emiliana
William of Wadington's *Manuel des Pechiez*
44 The knight who forgave his enemy
49 The backbiting monk

Life of St. Martin

5 St. Martin and the Devil
25 St. Martin's cloak

Life of St. Thomas

11 The birth of St. Thomas

Life of St. Marina

16 The monk " Mawryne "
Life of St. Eustace

18 St. Eustace
Life of St. Edmund

27 St. Edmund and the devil
Life of St. Theophilus

39 " Theophil "

Life of St. Pelagia

43 St. Pelagia
Life of St. Alexis

53 St. Alexis

Dialogus Miraculorum

13 The usurious knight
Nicole de Bozon's *Contes Moralizés* (?)
31 Carpus
Exempla ascribed to Jacques de Vitry
35 The hermit and the angel
A French Fabliau
38 The hermit and St. Oswald
Romance of Alexander (Ecclesiastical Latin version)
46 The imprisoned Jews
Jacques de Vitry or the *Alphabetum Narrationum*
55 The wise son

Paraldus' Summa virtutum ac vitiorum

32 The melancholy king (Damocles' sword theme)
No source found
8 The archbishop and the nun
15 The hermit who returned to the world

The fact that above twenty sources were utilized for the tales only, suggests no little industry on the part of the homilist. The list also indicates that the great thirteenth century continental storehouses, such as the *Legenda Aurea*, the *Dialogus Miraculorum*, the *Speculum Morale*, the *Summa virtutum ac vitiorum*, the *Alphabetum Narrationum*, and the exempla of Jacques de Vitry, were available in England by the opening of the fourteenth century.

Aside from the fact that saints' legends preponderate, and that local and contemporary incidents are wholly absent, this collection offers no unusual features. Appearances after death, the saving grace of the Virgin, the wiles of the devil incarnate, the evil deeds of laymen and clerics with their punishment or subsequent reformation through divine clemency, are ever-recurring themes. As usual, a number of particular mediaeval favorites appear; most notable among these are the following: the legend of Theophilus,[57] the pilgrim to St. James,[58] the prioress miraculously delivered,[59] St. Eustace,[60] the melancholy king,[61] the hermit and the angel.[62] Over and

[57] Gerould, *op. cit.*, 76–7–8, lists twenty-five Latin versions, about a dozen French, three English, and refers to German, Dutch, and Icelandic versions.

[58] This tale deals with a man who, on a pilgrimage, fell into deadly sin. Later he met the devil in the likeness of St. James. The devil commanded the man to mutilate and slay himself and then made off with the victim's soul, but was shortly confronted by St. Peter and St. James, who secured the intervention of the Virgin. Through her aid the man was restored to life and became a devout monk. Gerould (p. 31) states that this legend with slight variations is found " in almost innumerable collections of Mary legends, of exempla, and of pious treatises."

[59] The prioress sinned, and just before being subjected to trial, was miraculously delivered of a child through the intervention of the Virgin. Gerould (pp. 92–3–4) lists about twenty-five versions of this popular *conte dévot*.

[60] St. Eustace, as the reader may remember, was a sort of mediaeval Job, whose constancy in spite of a long series of persecutions, was a means of converting many heathen, according to the story.

[61] This analogue to the Damocles' sword story, came originally from *Barlaam and Josaphat*. Gerould (pp. 67–8) notes twenty-nine versions, varying in details. He also points out that the casket feature was detached from this legend and became the parent of the casket element in the *Merchant of Venice*.

[62] The hermit held his nose while passing a decaying corpse but his angel

over again, as I have indicated in the notes, were these and similar tales, copied in sermons, example-books, collections of tales, and didactic treatises. Measured by the supply, the demand must have been enormous.

The regular occurrence of the tales and their length in the *N. E. Homily Collection* show that the exemplum had secured a firm position in English sermons. The *Gesta Romanorum*, as well as other collections, had by this time been compiled in England, and had naturally added to the vogue of tales with a moral. However, the moderation and serious use made of the tales in these homilies, indicate a lingering of the conservatism which had hitherto characterized English preachers. The collection rarely has more than one tale in a sermon, and it is never trivial, never merely entertaining; the purpose is always earnest. For example, the writer states that man is sinful till he has Christ in his heart; then,

> "That may ye se aperteli,
> Wit mani ensampel witerly,
> Namly bi Mari Maudelayn."

After telling the story of Mary Magdalene, he recapitulates as follows:

> "This tal haf I tald you,
> To scheu on quat maner and hou,
> That quen Crist cumes intil our hertes,
> To lef our sin he us ertes,
> And geres us ask him forgivenes,
> Of al our sinnes mar and les."[63]

Again, the preacher warns sinners to beware the day of doom, for the day of judgment is to be terribly severe. The truth of this may be confirmed, he says, by an account "that falles wel til our godspelle."[64] Then follows the tale of the black monk

companion took no notice; later the angel, much to the astonishment of the hermit, held his nose at the sight of a fair young man riding by with a hawk on his wrist. Gerould (pp. 71–2) lists fourteen versions of this tale.

[63] *Eng. Metr. Hom.,* 15, 19.

[64] *Ibid., 29.* Small states (*ibid.,* 180) that Roger of Wendover's Chronicle (c. 1072) contains a similar account based on a supposedly actual happening at Nantes. This suggests the point already treated, that exempla were usually told as facts not fictions.

who returned from death and said that owing to a slight indiscretion he had only escaped punishment by the Virgin's intercession. The writer closes,

> " This tal haf I tald you,
> To schew on quat maner and hou
> We sal be demed, and yeld acount
> Quat our sinnes mai amount,
> For al sal com to rounge, I wis,
> Thar, that her mistakin isse
> Bi the lest idel thoht,
> For thar forgifnes bes riht noht."[65]

Similarly, in another place, he introduces the tale as follows:

> " Bot for I said that Satenas
> Waites us als thef in pas,
> I wille you tel of a pilgrim,
> Hou Satenas bigiled him."

The story closes,

> " Bi this tal har may we se,
> That wis and wair bihoves us be,
> That Satenas ne ger us rayk
> Fra rihtwisnes, to sinful laik."[66]

These typical passages show the insistence on the religious point of the exemplum. We are here far removed from the brief and occasional narratives of Old English tradition, but although the tales have greatly increased the attractiveness of the sermons, there is still an admirably serious motive behind them.

We come now to the *Contes Moralizés* of Nicole de Bozon, an English Franciscan who wrote his treatise in bad French[67]

---

[65] *Eng. Metr. Hom.*, 33.

[66] *Ibid.*, 53, 58. For similar introductions and conclusions, see pp. 68, 73, 78, 93, 111, 115, 130, 132, 138, 143, 148, 151, 163, 164, 170.

[67] *Contes Moralizés*, introd., lii–lxvi. Paul Meyer here speaks of the considerable use of French in England at the time of the *Contes,* even among the common people. E. Stengel notes a fourteenth century collection of Anglo-Norman exempla written in couplets. The majority of the tales are taken from the *Vitae Patrum* and Gregory's *Dialogues,* but a few come from the *Bible,* saints' lives, and local tradition. One tale, the compiler states, he heard " en sarmon." The nature of the collection may be seen from the following topics treated. No. 2 deals with chastity

shortly after 1320.[68] Although the work is not a regular set of
sermons, it was undoubtedly used as such. "Évidemment,"
says Paul Meyer, "c'est un livre qui a été prêché, et sans doute
plus d'une fois, avant d'être écrit. Le désordre qui se remar-
que dans l'arrangement des matières montre que nous sommes
en présence de morceaux rapidement rédigés, négligemment
rassemblés, où même quelques parties sont encore à l'état de
notes. Il n'y a pas, dans toute la littérature anglo-normande,
un second ouvrage qui puisse nous donner une idée aussi com-
plète de ce qu'était en Angleterre et au commencement du
XIVe siècle, la prédication populaire."[69] In its use of both
moralizations and narrative illustrations it is a very illuminating
document on the nature of popular preaching in England of the
fourteenth century, and is especially valuable because of the
extreme rarity of popular sermon collections extant.[70] I shall,
therefore, discuss the *Contes Moralizés* in some detail.

As I have already shown in speaking of the saints' lives and
the *N. E. Homilies,* which employed narratives so freely, traditional heaviness had given way in popular preaching to the
more attractive method of the friars. The *Contes Moralizés*
represents a variant form of the popular appeal, in the extrac-
tion of morals from minerals, plants, animals, popular beliefs
and superstitions. Dry allegorical interpretation of Scriptural
passages had been the traditional stronghold in sermon writing,
and even the "properties of things" had long since been occa-

in women; No. 7 with the value of alms-giving; Nos. 10 to 15 with confession; No. 20 with the sin of robbing the poor, which seems to have
been a besetting evil of the times; Nos. 23, 24, 27, with usury; No. 28
with the crime of killing for land; No. 32 with combating fleshly temptation; No. 34 with envy; No. 36 with the sin of singing "caroles" and
playing "luttes" in the church or cemetery. The tales are told for the
purpose of proving or illustrating the accompanying discussion. The most
frequent introductory expressions are, "Ceo vous proveroi par un count,"
or "Et ceo treis bien confermerai par un conte que vous conterai." *Zeit-
schrift für französische Sprache und Litteratur,* XIV, 129 seq.

[68] *Contes Moralizés,* introd., ii.

[69] *Contes Moralizés,* introd., xxviii. See also Philip Harry, *A Comparative Study of the Aesopic Fable in Nicole de Bozon,* 73.

[70] Meyer says "On possède plusieurs recueils d'homélies et de sermons
anglais du XIVe siècle, mais ils n'ont pas un caractère véritablement populaires." *Contes,* introd., xxviii, note.

sionally used as illustrations in sermons. In the *Contes Moralizés* these "properties of things" are systematically made the bases of the little treatises; a moral application follows; and to this is frequently added an exemplum. As in the case of Holkot's later *Liber Sapientiae,* which resembles the *Contes,* Biblical texts are freely sprinkled through the various parts. The contents of a typical chapter, or number, may be briefly outlined. The title, as always, is in Latin: "Quod multos excecat gaudium mundiale." The nature of the deer is to delight in melody. One hunter plays sweetly while another comes up and shoots. So, many people delight in worldly things and lose sight of the engines of evil. Then follows the customary Biblical citation, to the effect that fools are drawn by empty delights. The lesson is made concrete by the exemplum of the sad king and his brother (Damocles' sword theme). After the tale comes another Scriptural citation from Proverbs, which again points the moral of the story.[71] The hundred and forty-five chapters which constitute the collection are not all as fully developed as the above. Some lack the exemplum; in others the exemplum stands alone; some of the chapters are very brief, and crudely worded, with the idea, apparently, of leaving further development and polish to the user, who might expand the material into a sermon, or interpolate it into his own discourse.

The key-note of the whole compilation is attractiveness combined with utility. Nicole was in sympathy with the masses, and was thoroughly in touch with contemporary conditions. There is nothing of the mystic or of the stilted theologian about him. Naturally, in writing a theological work, he could not fail to treat such topics as the deadly sins, confession, contrition, penitence, the virtue of the mass, alms-giving, the miraculous power of the Virgin, and the love of Christ.[72] But his emphasis is laid upon religio-social matters. Covetousness, worldly church-officials, scheming lawyers, cheating bailiffs and

---

[71] *Contes Moralizés,* 58–9.

[72] See Nos. 13, 39, 41, 45, 58, 61, 62, 63, 77, 78, 79, 86, 90, 98, on these and similar subjects.

seneschals, the oppressive rich, and usury,[73] are subjects which again and again constitute the themes of Nicole's moralizations and exempla.

His treatment of these subjects shows skill in the application and adaptation of material, rather than in invention.[74] Nor was he a widely-read scholar. His borrowed material, consisting of ideas from natural history, fables and tales, is drawn from a limited range of sources. Although in describing the "properties of things" he cites Aristotle, Pliny, Dioscorides, St. Basilius, Isidor, Avicenna, and others, he did not consult the originals, but the *De Proprietatibus Rerum* of Bartholomaeus Anglicus or a similar work based upon the writings of the men mentioned.[75] The limitation of Nicole's scholarship is suggested by a curious error of attribution. In telling the story of the man chased by the unicorn, which comes from *Barlaam and Josaphat,* Nicole, thinking Barlaam to be the author, says, "Barleam conte en son livere."[76] For his fables, he had access to the work of Marie de France, the fables of Odo de Ceritona, and the *Disciplina Clericalis* from which he drew a part of one fable.[77] It is impossible to determine precisely the sources of the tales other than the fables, but it is fairly certain that Nicole made use of the exempla of Jacques de Vitry, Beda's *Ecclesiastical History,* a collection of *contes dévots, Vitae Patrum,* and the *Disciplina Clericalis.*[78]

[73] We get here an indication of that socialistic preaching which brought about in 1382 a statute of Richard II enjoining preachers who without license roamed about scattering seeds of dissention.

[74] " On retrouve des bestiaires et des lapidaires dans les vastes encyclopédies qui parurent nombreuses au XIIIᵉ siècle sous les titres *d'Image du monde*, de *Mappemonde*, de *Miroir du monde*, de *Petite philosophie*, de *Lumière des Laïques*, de *Nature des choses*, et de *Propriétés des choses*. Ces ouvrages, en latin et en français, en vers et en prose, théologiques, philosophiques, géographiques, scientifiques, sont en général des compilations sans originalité, dont les matériaux sont puisés à droite et à gauche, chez des auteurs sacrés et profanes ; Aristote, Pline, Solin, Isidore de Séville, Honorius d'Autun, l'Ancien et le Nouveau Testament, les Pères de l'Église, le Physiologus, Palladius, Isaac, Jacques de Vitry, etc." See Petit de Julleville, *Histoire de la Langue et de la Littérature française*, II, 174.

[75] *Contes Moralizés*, introd., vi seq.

[76] *Ibid.*, 46.

[77] See P. Harry, *op. cit.*, 71–2 ; see also *Les Fabulistes Latins*, IV, 98.

[78] *Contes Moralizés*, introd., xiii–xiv.

A few exempla give probable evidence of being local anecdotes, contemporary or traditional. One tale deals with three
"ribauds" whose names, "Hoket," "Croket," and "Loket"
fairly proclaim their local origin.[79] Another tale contains the
characters of "William Werldeschame" and his spouse
"Moalde Mikimisaunter."[80] The central thought of the tale
about the shrewd farm-hand is expressed in a crude English
quotation: "On yis ne trist me nout" said the hind, as he
scattered a handful of seeds over the ground; "Yis have I now
y-bouth," as he put some into his mouth.[81] Again, in the long
story of the devil's hunting-dogs, found elsewhere only in the
Gesta, the dogs have English names. Two "mauvais grace-
ons" in another tale are called "Sterlyn and Galopyn."[82] Inasmuch as the tales in which these names are found are largely
homely and secular, English origin is altogether likely. Certain other tales relate incidents involving prominent local persons, such as the Abbot of Westminster and Henry III,[83] John
of Alderby, the Bishop of Lincoln,[84] and Ralph Baron.[85]
Though few, the local and particularly the secular narratives,[86]
give Nicole's work a slight flavor of freshness if not of
originality.

The fable and the time-honored monkish legend, however,
dominate the narrative portion. The fable lent itself particularly to the illustration of social defects, and the moralized
fables of Odo de Ceritona and Alexander Neckam had admirably pointed the way for Nicole. No less than thirty-seven
fables do duty as exempla in the *Contes Moralizés,* usually

[79] *Contes Moralizés,* 137.

[80] *Ibid.,* 166. Meyer points out in the notes (pp. 288–89) that "Worldly-
Shame" appears in the interlude, *Nice Wanton.*

[81] *Ibid.,* 110.

[82] *Ibid.,* 180.

[83] Ibid., 85.

[84] *Ibid.,* 181.

[85] *Ibid.,* 63. The knight, Ralph Baron, according to the story, was aided
at his death-bed by the Virgin, and restored to a life thenceforth devoted
to good deeds.

[86] At the opening of the fourteenth century, as I mentioned in speaking
of the *Gesta,* tales of a more secular nature were coming into vogue with
churchmen.

under the title of " Fabula ad Idem." The other exempla, frequently distinguished by the title of " Narracio ad Idem," are slightly less numerous. The majority of these are monkish anecdotes and episodes from the saints' lives, now rising to the height of their popularity. The following are notable favorites used in the collection: the hermit and the angel; the melancholy king, the true son (test for legitimacy), Beda's tale of Ymma and Tunna, the monk who returned after three hundred years, the holy man who resisted temptation by burning his fingers.[87] Such well-known tales are representative of the exempla as distinguished from the fables of the treatise. Except in his unusually frequent use of fables, local and secular anecdotes, Nicole does not differ materially from his contemporaries who got the attention of the masses by appealing to their love for stories, their veneration for authority, their vulgarity, ignorance and credulity.

In spite of the increasing vogue of story-telling among popular preachers at the middle of the fourteenth centry, few traces of it appear in the writings of one important group of religious writers, the Mystics. It is undoubtedly true that the English Mystics, under the influence of Bonaventura, were, like the friars, practical in their work and methods; moreover, they were antagonistic to scholasticism.[88] But their discourses differ sufficiently from those of the Franciscan-Dominican school to require some notice of the popular work of a thoroughgoing representative, Richard Rolle.

This man, although he did not belong to a monastic order, and, being neither priest nor in holy orders, could not occupy the pulpit,[89] nevertheless mingled with the masses, taught the glory of divine love, and expounded the Scripture, the creed, the church offices, the vices and virtues.[90] But in the work of Rolle and his followers the exemplum is not as prominent as in the other fourteenth century writings which we have con-

[87] *Contes Moralizés,* 50, 58, 71, 101, 112, 118, respectively.

[88] See Horstmann, *Richard Rolle and his Followers,* I, introd., xii–xiii.

[89] *Richard Rolle and his Followers,* I, introd., x.

[90] Perry speaks of Rolle as a " traveling preacher, intensely devoted to the work of the instruction of his fellow creatures." See *English Prose Treatises of Richard Rolle de Hampole,* preface, xiii.

sidered. The more earnest tone of Wycliffe is prefigured. This difference of method is not due to a change of audience or of aim. Rolle writes, as he says in the *Pricke of Conscience,*

> " For to stirre lewed men til mekenes,
> And to make þam luf God and drede."[91]

The popular treatise just mentioned has but one clear-cut exemplum, and the same scarcity of narrative illustrations is to be noted in the prose treatises. Here and there a brief, irregularly placed narrative reference or anecdote appears. These are almost all taken from the *Bible,* Gregory's *Dialogues, Vitae Patrum,* and the *Dialogus Miraculorum,* with an occasional citation from *Barlaam and Josaphat,* the *Life of St. Richard,* and the *Life of St. Augustine.* The score of developed exempla found among the prose treatises are used with perfect recognition of the type, being termed " narracio " or " exemplum."[92] But the infrequency of their appearance here shows that the narrative element, although pervasive, did not wholly dominate popular preaching during the fourteenth century. There were at least a few men so intense in promoting the higher, purer life, that they avoided the exemplum which too often " smelled of mortality."

Meanwhile, in spite of detractors, the exemplum increased in vogue as the century drew to a close. Wycliffe, as has been stated, bitterly denounced those who " techen opynly fablys, cronyklis and lesyngis and leven cristis gospel and þe maundements of god."[93] The practice against which Wycliffe inveighed was in great measure due to the roving friars, whose unrecorded sermons doubtless contained more tales than are retained in the written specimens at our disposal. The final collection which we shall examine, however, John Mirk's *Festial,* fairly indicates the height of popularity reached by the type at the opening of the fifteenth century.

[91] *The Pricke of Conscience,* 258. As I shall point out in the following chapter, exempla were prominent in treatises of this kind during the fourteenth century.

[92] For exempla, see *Richard Rolle and his Followers,* I, 12–13, 139, 140, 141, 143, 144, 152, 192–93, 194, 333.

[93] *The English Works of Wycliffe,* 16. For similar expressions, see above p. 17.

Mirk, a canon of Lilleshull in Shropshire, wrote, besides the *Festial,* a *Manuale Sacerdotum* and an English poem, *Instructions for Parish Priests,* which he translated from the *Pupilla Oculi* of William de Pagula.[94] The *Instructions* teaches clerical duties and exhorts the clergy to lead strict, clean lives; in every way, it seems to indicate that Mirk, though merely the translator, was among the better class of preachers. A liberal use of tales by such a man is suggestive of excesses on the part of the rank and file whom Wycliffe denounced,—men who were sometimes more intent upon lining their own pockets than saving benighted souls.

In the seventy-four sermons constituting Mirk's *Festial,* we have complete union of the homilies "de sanctis" and the homilies "de tempore," thus providing a cycle for the whole year. Forty of the sermons belong to the former group and the remaining thirty-four to the latter. The discourses for saints' days are the usual loosely-joined sequences of events in the lives of various saints, with the addition of distinctly indicated exempla of much the same tenor. The Sunday sermons begin with a story from the Bible, such as that of Moses and the tablets of stone, or Joseph and his brethren, told in simple form. The writer then explains the lesson to be drawn from the Scripture, and usually closes with two or more exempla. Occasionally a brief "signification" of some bit of Biblical narrative recalls the heavy symbolism of the early school,[95] but traces of the ponderous and scholarly exegesis of St. Augustine, Gregory, Jerome, and Beda, are comparatively few.[96] Nature allegories and entertaining narratives with a moral predominate in this prominent model sermon-book of the early fifteenth century.

[94] See Miss Bateman's article in *D. N. B.*

[95] For example, the feeding of the multitude is explained as follows: "The first loaf of these five is contrition of heart. The second is true shrift of mouth. The third is retribution for trespass. The fourth is fear of relapsing into sin. The fifth is perseverance in God. The two fishes are prayer and alms-deed." *Festial,* I, 103; see also pp. 96, 228–32, for more elaborate instances.

[96] References to St. Augustine are most numerous; see *ibid.,* 45, 55, 56, 169, 192, 231.

Wherever the body of the sermon is not narrative in form, it consists of an explanation of the festival to be celebrated, or of a set of exhortations to obey various divine laws for certain plainly-stated reasons. The definiteness of appeal is increased by a feature much employed by the schoolmen,— the use of specific numbers, of which "three" is particularly favored. For example, men "synnen in þre wayes," the Church hallows St. Paul's conversion "for þre skylles," the Church to-day worships the Virgin "specyaly yn þre þynges," "Holy Chyrche . . . ordeyned þre maner of salvys to hele hur chyldren wyþ," Christ will pardon sinful men if they have "þre þyngys þat ben nedefull to hom."[97] To teach effectively, in accordance with ecclesiastical interpretation, the ideal Christian life, to emphasize the orthodox means to that end, viz., contrition, shrift, penance, alms-giving, and the like, and to hold up the saints as models of excellence,—these are the aims admirably kept in view, whether we smile indulgently at the writer's naïve enumerations, or deprecate the profusion of illustrative tales which sprinkle his pages.

Mirk, adopting the popular method, disregarded strictures upon the exemplum, just as he did the outcries against the use of crosses and images.[98] But although his sermons contain, exclusive of the incidents related as a part of the saints' lives, no less than one hundred and six exempla, he appears never to forget that the tales are told for their lessons and not merely for the purpose of entertainment. He states that he has no sympathy with a "tale of rybawdy,"[99] and in a sermon directed to priests, he warns them to "be war of spekyng rybawdy"; to impress the caution he tells of the terrible fate of "a prest yn Yerlond þat was lusty to speke of rybawdy and iapys þat turned men to lechery."[100] An exemplum was, how-

[97] *Festial*, I, 150, 53, 57, 64, 74, resp. References to this and other numbers might be multiplied.

[98] "Herefor ben roodes sett on hey in holy chirch, and so by syȝt þerof have mynd of Cristis passion. And þerfor roodes and oþyr ymages ben necessary in holy chirch, whatever þes Lollardes sayn; for yf þay nade ben profitable, goode holy faders þat have ben tofore us wold have don hem out of holy chirch mony a ȝere gon." *Festial*, I, 171.

[99] *Ibid.*, 156.

[100] *Ibid.*, 192.

ever, often essential to clearness. "But ӡet," he says, "for
þat mony wyttys ben lat and hevy forto leve þat þay may not
here ny se, but þay be broght yn by ensampull. For þogh þe
ensampull be not most comendabull, ӡet for þe more parte hit
may soo lyghten his wyt, þat he may þe sondyr come to beleve."[101] Why should he not use exempla? Not only had
numerous eminent churchmen from the time of Gregory the
Great sanctioned their use, but, as Mirk points out before telling the parable of the sower, "God techythe by ensampull."[102]
As we shall see, Mirk's exempla are often far removed in kind
from the parables, but he did pretty consistently try to keep it
clear that the tales were a means, not an end. As a rule they
bear directly upon the point at issue, and are introduced by the
usual proposal to confirm an assertion, to illustrate an observation, to stimulate devotion,[103] or to stir up the conscience. A
restatement of the lesson involved usually follows the narrative.

But exempla had, by 1400, become much more numerous
and elaborate than mere utility would warrant. The end of
the discourse had long been established as the logical place for
tales and though not always strictly adhered to,[104] this custom
generally prevailed. Owing to the popularity of stories, however, their number and length had steadily increased. Whereas
we found one tale closing each homily of the *North English
Collection*, we frequently have two, three, or four, at the end of
Mirk's discourses.[105] At times they are brief outlines[106] as
found in the example-books, but usually they are completely
rounded stories, developed with considerable attention to details
and occupying from half a page to two pages of the text. The
narratives are, generally speaking, of greater bulk than the
exegetical portions.

[101] *Festial*, I, 166.

[102] *Ibid.*, 71.

[103] Among the sermons "de sanctis" this is particularly common; for
typical instances, see *Festial*, 26, 158, 180, 189.

[104] Mirk occasionally uses an exemplum in the midst of a sermon.

[105] For example, No. 14 has three; No. 17 has four; No. 20 has three;
No. 24 has three; No. 40 has four; No. 41 has five; No. 50 has three;
No. 53 has three; No. 65 has four.

[106] See *Festial*, 220, 280.

The *Festial* is also indicative of the great latitude which preachers still exercised in illustrative tales. Though Mirk is sparing of the more offensive "tales of rybawdy" so common in Latin collections and in the work of such men as Nicole de Bozon, he has no hesitation in narrating as facts the most absurd fabrications. Unlike Aelfric, he affirms the bodily assumption of the Virgin, on the authority of a revelation to St. Elizabeth of Spain.[107] More in evidence than ever before are the troops of fiends clawing at the souls of expiring sinners; more swelling is the chorus of wailing voices from belated penitents immured in marble images or cakes of ice; more bewildering are the astounding rescues by wonder-working saints. Specific references become superfluous when almost every page abounds in things never heard or witnessed on land or sea. The popular English preacher, with the best of intentions no doubt, has become a *raconteur* of marvels.

Exempla were taken from a widening variety of sources, though *contes dévots* and saints' lives, especially those of the *Legenda Aurea,* were now more prominent than ever. In a number of instances Mirk has stated his sources, which I cite; but they are by no means exhaustive:[108] Lives of St. Edward the Confessor, St. Dunstan, St. Dominick, St. Brandan, St. Winfred, St. Fylbert, St. Sylvester, St. Richard, St. George, St. Carpeus, St. Remus, St. Gregory, St. Odo of Canterbury, St. Guthlac, St. Margaret;[109] Works of Beda, St. Augustine, Alexander Neckam, Josephus, Melitus, the Bible, Ranulf Higden's Polychronicon, "Gestes" of the Romans, Dialogues of Gregory, Acts of the Apostles, Vitae Patrum, "Gestes" of France, Legenda Aurea, "þe mayster of stories,"[110] John

---

[107] *Festial*, 226. Perhaps he guards himself by remarking at the close of the passage, "þus clerkys preven how our lady was assumpted bodely ynto Heven."

[108] A study of the sources and analogues of Mirk's exempla offers a fruitful subject for research, although Dr. Erbe's promised second volume may undertake the matter.

[109] Mirk may have consulted the *Legenda Aurea* for some of these.

[110] The tale referred to this source deals with King Darius' question as to which is strongest: wine, women, or a king. It is told by Gower, *Conf. Amant.*, Bk. VII, ll. 1783 seq.

Belet.[111]   Many of the tales have no reference to their source
other than "I rede" or "I finde," but the above list is sufficient to indicate the kind of narratives favored. We see that
later and secular sources, together with saints' lives, were
growing in favor, and that patristic writings and the mediaeval
exempla collections were decreasing in popularity.

Many tales in the *Festial* deal with local happenings and are,
apparently, set down from oral tradition. These are suggestive of the way in which exempla sprang up, but the local
tales throw scarcely more light upon men and ideas of the times
than do those of universal application.[112]   Nevertheless, it
is quite likely that they were doubly effective on contemporary
audiences. So Mirk must have calculated when, for instance,
he says in introducing the story of a sinner torn to pieces by
three dogs, "Wherefor I telle þis ensampull þat was told me
of suche þat knewyn hit done yn dede."[113]   Similarly, he gives
an account of a company of fellows taking a "stene of ale"
to drink in a tavern. Among the number was a priest who,
strangely enough, recalled that a clerical duty awaited him.
Being requested to bless the ale before leaving, he complied,
whereupon the "stene barste al to pesus, and a grete tode was
in þe stene boþom." This also was "a tale þat was don in
dede."[114]   Some of these tales center about prominent national
figures. For example, he narrates how Thomas à Becket and
King Henry II, while riding together "yn þe Chepe of London" on a cold day, met a thinly clad man. Becket was wear-
ing a cloak "of fyne scarlad, well yfurred wyþ grys." This
the king seized and after they had "wrastlet long," Becket let

[111] John Belet appears to have been an Englishman who was at one time
a theologian in Paris. Migne (*Patr. Lat.*, CCII) prints his *Rationale
divinorum officiorum*, and calls him "Theologus Parisiensis." Belet is cred-
ited also with a collection of sermons and a treatise entitled *Gemma
Animae*. See *D. N. B.*

[112] It is interesting to note the emphasis upon such topics as lechery,
revellings, gluttony, vain plays at Christmas time, and the desirability of
submitting to earthly trials for the sake of a proportionate reward in
heaven. But these things were, of course, not peculiar to England.

[113] *Festial*, I, 56.

[114] *Ibid.*, 293.

him pull it off and cast it to the poor man. The prelate simulated anger but was really well content.[115] Another tale deals with "Robert Grosched, Byschop of Lyncolne." It seems that to his death-bed came "a gret multytude of fendys, and spyted wyþ hym so of þe fayþe, þat þay hadden negh turned hym." But "oure lady," ever ready, said to him, "say þou belevyst as holy chyrch doþe." Robert hastened to reply, "Y beleve as holy chyrch belevyþ," whereat the fiends vanished and he gave up the ghost in peace.[116] Many other wonderful happenings are located by the homilist in various parts of England, notably as follows: a miracle was witnessed by two men dwelling near Norwich; a wonderful miracle happened in Devonshire "bysyde Auxbryge"; a miracle happened to a man of "Erkaleton" named Adam; a miraculous cure was wrought in the town of Shrewsbury; an unshriven man near the "abbay of Lulsull" was tormented after death; a child near Northampton had visions of the punishment of an adulterous man; the Virgin appeared in the nunnery of Shaftesbury and urged fewer "aves" and more devotion.[117] These tales, aside from the fact that they have "a local habitation and a name," are scarcely different from the great mass of monkish legends which had been circulating for centuries throughout the Christian realm. This bears witness to the fact that anything like distinct national features in religious literature was practically impossible under an organization so universal and all-powerful as the mediaeval Church.[118] Mirk's effort to infuse new material and to localize the exemplary incidents is practically lost amid the mass of well-worn tales which play so important a

[115] *Festial,* I, 39-40.

[116] *Ibid.,* 78.

[117] *Ibid.,* 91, 173, 180, 181, 192, 281, 293, 299, resp.

[118] "In the fourteenth century," says W P. Ker, "one need not be surprised to find that a good deal of the prose of all the countries of Europe is a little monotonous and jaded. For the general character of progress had been a levelling down of national distinctions, and a distribution over the whole field of the same commonplaces, so that one finds the same books current everywhere, the same stories; the popular learning in the vernacular tongues became almost as clear of any national or local character as the philosophy of the schools." *Essays on Mediaeval Literature,* 21.

part in this representative of English preaching at the time of Chaucer, Langland, Gower and Wycliffe.

To summarize,—we have seen that at the opening of the thirteenth century exempla in Latin were circulating among the clergy but preaching was at a low ebb, and stories were rarely employed in the dry sermons of the period. Then, toward the close of the first quarter of the century, came the friars, who spread quickly through the thickly settled districts and popularized the tales in their vernacular sermons. During the remainder of the century, however, the exemplum was little used in English. Meanwhile, saints' lives had been accumulating and growing in favor, and by the opening of the fourteenth century were circulating widely. The legendary had now to a certain extent taken the place of the ordinary homilies, especially in the service for saints' days. Narratives in the pulpit were thus encouraged both by the sermons of the friars and by readings from the legendaries. About 1300 the *North English Homily Collection* gave prominent expression in the vernacular to the exemplum. A little later the *Contes Moralizés* of Nicole de Bozon, in addition to their use of tales, sometimes local and secular, indicate that fables and moralizations from nature and popular superstitions were in vogue as material for sermons. The treatises of Richard Rolle and his followers show that among the Mystics, narration was distinctly subordinate to the expression of thought and religious emotion. Finally, at the opening of the fifteenth century, Mirk's *Festial* represents the type at the height of favor. Secular tales mingle in profusion with episodes from saints' lives and monkish legends and though evidently serious in his aims, the preacher has become a teller of tales rather than an expounder of the gospel.

The exemplum had taken such strong hold upon both preachers and people that it maintained itself for a long time in spite of opposition. Wycliffe and his followers had, in the closing years of the fourteenth century, voiced a strong objection to the use of tales in the pulpit, but a confirmed practice which lightened the labors of the clergy and pleased the masses was not to be stopped at once. Even the opposition of the

Church Councils, as was pointed out in the introductory chapter, failed for a time to do more than check the abuse of illustrative tales. So the use of exempla continued in England, as elsewhere, and new translations of Latin example-books appeared. Sermon collections of the fifteenth and sixteenth centuries attest the persistence of the type[119] and show that even such reformers as Latimer[120] were not altogether beyond its pervasive influence. By 1400, however, the beginning of the end had arrived; the Reformation had set in and although the decline was gradual, the passing of the exemplum was foreshadowed.[121]

[119] See Crane, *J. de V.*, introd., liii; also Douce, *Illustrations of Shakspere*, II, 341–42.

[120] See *Sermons by Hugh Latimer*. It is important to note that Latimer's narratives usually resemble more the illustrations used by modern preachers than they do the legendary incidents which made the exemplum a distinct type.

[121] Cf. Paul's *Grundriss*, II, Pt. ii, 739.

CHAPTER V

THE EXEMPLUM IN RELIGIOUS TREATISES AND INSTRUCTION-BOOKS

In addition to its use in sermons, the exemplum was employed in at least two other types of literature, the religious treatise and the instruction-book, which constitute the subject of this chapter.

Inasmuch as the religious treatises consist of discussions of the vices, virtues and kindred topics pertaining to ecclesiastical discipline, they closely resemble the sermons. It was a Church policy to expound regularly the commandments, the creed, the virtues, and the deadly sins. A ruling of the Synod of Oxford (1281) ordered that "every priest having charge of a flock, do, four times in each year (that is, once each quarter), on one or more solemn feast days, either himself or by some one else, instruct the people in the vulgar language, simply and without any fantastical admixture of subtle distinctions, in the Articles of the Creed, the Ten Commandments, the Evangelical Precepts, the Seven Works of Mercy, the Seven Deadly Sins with their Offshoots, the Seven Principal Virtues, and the Seven Sacraments."[1] Instruction of this sort was not confined to sermons; treatises helped to spread the knowledge of how to live so as to gain the reward of heaven. I have already cited the *English Metrical Homilies* to the effect that

[1] See Gasquet, *Parish Life in Mediaeval England*, 214; also 215, for a similar ruling. In 1357 Archbishop Thoresby of York had Jon Gatryke, a monk of St. Mary's, York, translate into English an exposition of the creed, commandments, virtues, sins, etc. The Archbishop says in his preface to the tract that it is sent out to all his priests "so that each and every one, who under him had the charge of souls, do openly in English, upon Sundays teach and preach them, that they have cure of the law and the way to know God Almighty." *Parish Life*, 216. The Synod of Ely (1364) ordered that every priest frequently expound the ten commandments, etc., in English. *Ibid.*, 216.

> " . . . Laued men havis mar mister,
> Godes word for to her
> Than klerkes that thair mirour lokes,
> And sees hou thai sal lif on bokes."[2]

About 1200, when this was written, "mirours" for the laity began to appear in English.

One of the earliest of these treatises extant is the Middle English dialogue between Soul and Reason, entitled *Vices and Virtues*. Since this piece illustrates in its plan the type with which we are to deal, it may be briefly outlined. First, Soul, representing mankind, indicates the vices to which she is addicted: sorrow, sloth, pride,[3] disobedience, swearing, lying, backbiting, deceit, cursing, impatience, self-will, unrighteousness, the ill-doing of the five senses. Reason suggests betterment by advising right-belief, firm hope, charity, humility, fear, pity, knowledge, counsel, strength, understanding and wisdom. But other virtues are desirable to perfect Soul in her progress, so after an interruption, Reason continues to prescribe peace, prudence, foresight, righteousness, moderation, obedience, mercy, penitence, confession, cleanness in body and thought, discipline, patience, maidenhood, chastity, continence, innocence, abstinence, fasting, sobriety, conscience, prayer, tears, discretion, and perseverance. This list indicates how thoroughly the Church had classified the vices and virtues of humanity and provided that the good should serve as an antidote for the evil.[4] Nothing could be better adapted to the use of exempla than a treatise of this kind.

But in this early piece, as in some later ones of the same

---

[2] *Eng. Metr. Hom.*, 3. The number of such treatises in Latin must have been enormous. The translator of the *Orologium Sapientiae or the Seven Poyntes of Trewe Wisdom* says, "Þer beþ so manye bokes & tretees of vyces & vertues & of dyvers doctrynes, þat þis schort lyfe schalle have anende of anye manne þanne he maye owþere studye hem or rede hem." *Anglia*, X, 328.

[3] A note in the MS. follows "pride," to the effect that "envy" seems to have been overlooked by Soul. *V. and V.*, 6.

[4] It will be recalled that at the opening of the thirteenth century, the Church under Innocent III reached its supreme dominion over Christendom. Its influence was felt even upon the most insignificant acts of the people.

nature, the exemplum is negligible.[4a] The allegorical structure, which commonly characterized these pieces, is also but little emphasized. The writer states that Soul is God's temple. Right-belief is the foundation; the posts which are to bear up the edifice are such major virtues as humility, fear, knowledge, strength, and understanding; charity is the enclosing wall; to it are fastened the rafters, i. e., the other virtues. Steadfast hope is the roof which covers all beneath it with the shingles of holy thoughts which Wisdom, the work-master of the blessed temple, dictates.[5] This scheme, however, is not developed in the body of the treatise. In another early thirteenth century representative of the "mirour" type, *Sawle Warde,*[6] the exemplum is wanting but the allegorical scheme is enlarged. Here, Soul is a house of which Wit is the master, and Will the untoward wife. The servants of the house are of two kinds: first, the five senses needing ever to be guarded from following the directions of the lady of the house; second, Wit's four daughters, the virtues, Prudence, Spiritual Strength, Moderation, and Righteousness, each of which has special offices.

The Latin *Speculum of St. Edmund,* written by Archbishop Edmund Rich, who died in 1240, was translated into English[7] during the opening years of the second half of the century. Here again, the seven deadly sins, the seven Christian virtues, the ten commandments, the twelve articles of the creed, the seven works of mercy and the seven prayers of the Paternoster are set forth. The translator preserves the stern Manichean style of the author who held " sykerly þat it es a foule lychery for to delyte þe in rymes, and slyke gulyardy."[8] Beyond a doubt he would have looked upon the exemplum as savoring of "gulyardy"; at any rate the severity of the work is not relieved by allegory or exempla.

[4a] A brief exemplum from *Vitae Patrum,* illustrative of discretion, is the only instance. See *V. and V.,* 148.

[5] *Ibid.,* 92–4.

[6] Printed in *Old Eng. Hom.,* First Series. The source of the work is a piece by Hugo of Saint Victor. See *Engl. Stud.,* XII, 459–63; see also Vollhardt, *op. cit.,* 26 seq.

[7] Printed in *Religious Pieces in Prose and Verse,* ed. Perry.

[8] *Speculum,* 35.

The mid-fourteenth century treatise on the virtues and religious functions, called the *Abbey of the Holy Ghost*,[9] is less severe, inasmuch as it developed with an elaborate allegorical apparatus which probably made the book fairly inviting. Its general character may be recalled. The Abbey is builded on the River of Tears and its walls are made by Obedience and Mercy. The stones, which are Deeds of Charity, are cemented by Love of God and Right-faith. Patience and Strength raise the pillars; Prayer, the chapel; Contemplation, the dormitory; Pity, the infirmary; Devotion, the cellar; Meditation, the storehouse. The Holy Ghost rules the convent, and Charity is the abbess; Wisdom is the prioress, and Meekness, the subprioress. So the treatise runs on through the gamut of the virtues and religious functions of mediaeval daily life. This allegorical structure gave to the work a popular tone, but of the more diverting feature, the illustrative tale, there is little use. Traces of it here and there show at least an acquaintanc with the type. Reference is made to the familiar tale from the life of St. Bartholomew concerning the fiend who cried out, "Bartholmee incendunt me oraciones tue."[10] In another place appears a brief account from St. Augustine, of a priest who fell into a state of ravishment whenever the name of God was mentioned.[11] But the writer was distinctly of the Mystic cult, and as I previously pointed out, the Mystics were not inclined to use exempla. The contemporary manual translated by Jon Gatryke,[12] although it is a "Lay Folks Catechism" as well as a preachers' guide, has no illustrative tales. The explanation for the absence of exempla in the above treatises is, first, that they were based upon Latin treatises which did not contain exempla; second, some of the more dignified of the secular clergy were apparently unwilling to popularize their works by using the favorite means of their rivals, the friars. The exemplum, it must be remembered, was never quite free from reproach.

But sufficient evidence remains to show that some writers

---

[9] Printed in *Religious Pieces in Prose and Verse*.

[10] *Ibid.*, 52.

[11] *Ibid.*, 56.

[12] See above, p. 115, note.

looked upon the exemplum as a helpful adjunct in confirming and explaining the points in these "mirours," and as a legitimate temptation to read their otherwise dry pages. This will appear in the examination of the following treatises: William of Wadington's *Manuel des Pechiez,* with Robert of Brunne's adaptation, *Handlyng Synne* (1303), the *Aȝenbite of Inwyt* (1340), *Jacob's Well* (early 15th century), the *Myroure of Oure Ladye* (c. 1425).

Of William of Wadington, the author of the *Manuel,*[13] little is known beyond the fact that he was a thirteenth century cleric who

> ". . . en engletere fu ne,
> E norri, ordine, et aleve."[14]

This he urges in excuse of the bad French and somewhat crabbed versification of his treatise. It is quite likely that if Robert of Brunne had not made a redaction of the *Manuel* it would have remained in oblivion. As it is, the work has the modest distinction of being, so far as I can ascertain, the first vernacular "mirour" treatise in England to employ the exemplum consistently.[15] In substance, the work follows closely the lines noted in the opening pages of this chapter. Indeed, William disavows any invention and appears to take the usual mediaeval pride in assuring his readers that all is said on authority.[16] The purpose of the book is, he says, to enable people to amend their lives, but he suggests that the reading will be made enjoyable by tales:

> "Ki plus en lisant seit delituz,
> Cuntes vus mettrum nus aucuns,
> Sicum les seinz nus unt cunté,
> Pur plus fere hayr pechié."[17]

These tales, of which there are fifty-four, do not differ in sub-

---

[13] *Robert of Brunne's Handlyng Synne, with the French Treatise on which it was founded, Le Manuel des Pechiez by William of Wadington,* ed. by Furnivall for the Roxb. Club, 1862; re-ed. by Furnivall for the E. E. T. S., No. 114–23, to which I refer unless otherwise noted.

[14] *Roxb. ed.,* 413.

[15] Schofield (*op. cit.,* 463) dates it 1267.

[16] *Handlyng Synne,* 3.

[17] *Ibid.,* 4.

ject-matter and treatment from those in the sermons. Stories taken directly or indirectly from Gregory's *Dialogues,* the *Vitae Patrum, Acta Sanctorum,* saints' lives, Beda's *History,* and the *Bible* are most prominent. They are placed, regularly, near or at the close of the topic divisions. Secular and local tales are comparatively few. Here and there among the well-known exempla may be found unfamiliar ones, such as that of the adulterous wife whose skeleton was discovered split in two with a dragon lying between,[18] or of a proud lady whose ever renewing body was repeatedly burned to ashes by a fiery wheel.[19] But these themes indicate no departure from the established type. All of the stories are nearly as long as those in the *Metrical Homilies,* which they closely resemble.

Robert of Brunne's adaptation of the *Manuel* brings the exemplum nearer the realm of art than any work previously considered. In view of the fact that Robert produced the *Handlyng Synne* as early as 1303, he shows unusual ability as a story-teller; he has, moreover, a worthy aim.[20] Since

> "... many ben of swyche manere,
> þat talys and rymys wyl bleþly here;
> Yn gamys, & festys, & at þe ale,
> Love men to lestene trotevale:
> þat may falle ofte to vylanye,
> To dedly synne, or oþer folye,"[21]

Robert will supply them with tales which, if they "falle ofte to vylayne," at any rate have a corrective effect. A new audience is appealed to; not the audience which assembled to hear the preacher, though overlapping was, no doubt, considerable, but the assembly at "gamys, & festys, & at þe ale." The effect

---

[18] *Handlyng Synne,* 63 seq.

[19] *Ibid.,* 113 seq.

[20] Hearne, in his preface to Robert's redaction of Langtoft's *Chronicle,* says that Robert of Brunne "was of a chearfull, pleasant humour, and ... very blithe and merry whenever he saw a proper occasion; at all which times, however, he behav'd himself without any immoral or indecent expressions. He was naturally addicted to virtue, and his being engaged in a religious course of life made him have a stricter guard upon himself." *Roxb. ed.,* preface, xxxv.

[21] *Handlyng Synne,* 3.

of this on the spread and popularity of these moral tales must
have been great.

Robert makes no claim to originality,[22] but aside from almost
constant variations from his source,[23] his omissions and additions are numerous. Realizing that for his purpose too much
unrelieved religious matter would be ill-advised, he omitted
entirely the section on the Twelve Articles of Faith, the " Petit
Sermun " of six hundred and eighty-eight lines on the Fear of
God and the Love of God, and the final fourteen hundred and
sixty lines on the Over-scrupulous Conscience and the Efficacy
of Prayer.[24] In spite of the omissions, *Handlyng Synne* has
above three thousand lines more than the *Manuel,* at the point
where the adaptation ends. This increase is due in part to the
more flowing style of Robert; in part to his frequent amplification of moral precepts, but chiefly to the addition of illustrative
tales. Besides expanding some of those in the *Manuel,* Robert
adds no fewer than a dozen outright.[25] Some of these deal
with conventional themes, but even in them the treatment is so
spontaneous and fresh that the dry example-book versions are
not suggested. Most of the added tales, however, narrate local
events of which Robert knew or had heard. Such tales as
those of the witch and her cow-sucking bag, Robert Grosseteste
and why he loved music, the Cambridgeshire miser-parson, the
dishonest Kesteven executors, the reproof that a Norfolk bond-
man gave a knight, have a local, unconventional stamp both in
matter and manner.[26] But aside from these local tales, the
illuminating and poignant descriptions, the cleverly phrased
direct discourse, and the delightful interspersed personal
observations of the narrator, make even the hackneyed themes
live again.[27]

The *Handlyng Synne,* therefore, marks another distinct step
in the development of the type in England. The religious

[22] *Handlyng Synne,* 4.
[23] The parallel texts in both editions make comparison easy.
[24] These are printed in the *Roxb. edition.*
[25] See *ibid.,* preface, xv, for a list of these.
[26] For the above tales, see *Handlyng Synne,* 19, 158, 200, 206, 273, resp.
[27] Furnivall speaks of Robert as "the worthiest forerunner of Chaucer."
Roxb. ed., preface, iv; see also Schofield, *op. cit.,* 411–16.

treatise naturally gave greater opportunity than the more compact sermon for the amplification of illustrative narratives, but the exempla of the contemporary *Metrical Homilies* show an almost equal length. Robert went a step farther. Although he introduced and closed his tales with the familiar expressions,[28] he threw an added emphasis upon the story for the story's sake.[29] Often where a brief exemplum of the conventional pulpit variety would have been logically more perspicuous, he tells an elaborate tale which in spite of its moral is distinctly entertaining and has a beginning, middle and end. Robert of Brunne advances the type toward Gower in whose hands it becomes detached from its ecclesiastical moorings.

The next work which we shall consider, the *Aȝenbite* of *Inwyt,* though it did not appear till 1340, is distinctly inferior to the *Handlyng Synne.* The *Aȝenbite,* as is well known, is a translation by the Augustinian monk, Dan Michel, of Frere Lorenz's *Le Somme des Vices et des Vertues,* composed in 1279. Dan Michel, instead of popularizing his original, translated literally, and the result is almost if not quite as heavy as the contemporary *Pricke of Conscience.* Barring a few exempla,[30] the only relief from its dry explanation of commandments, articles of belief, sins and virtues, is its curious system of allegorical nomenclature. As may be remembered, the seven deadly sins are here represented as seven heads of the "beste of helle;" each head has a number of "boughs" which in some cases have "twigs." The virtues are divided into "boughs" and "steps." Among all this forest of vices and virtues, there are seven comparatively bright places, the exempla.

---

[28] A typical opening and closing may be cited:

> "And þat may wel preved be
> Wyþ a tale of auctoryte.
> ....
> ....
> By þys ensample may ȝe see
> þat god ys ever ful of pyte." *Hand. Syn., 7, 12.*

[29] It will be remembered that at about this time the *Gesta Romanorum* did something similar for example-books.

[30] The exempla had appeared in the original; cf. Petit de Julleville, *op. cit.,* II, 182.

But the exempla take us back from the spirited tales of Robert to the example-book style. For instance, to illustrate how severely blasphemy is liable to be punished, Dan Michel says: "There was a knight that swore by God's eyes. Quickly one of his eyes leaped upon the chess-board. An archer, because he had lost at gaming, took his arrow and shot upwards toward God. That morning when he sat gaming, his arrow fell upon the chess-board all bloody."[31] Another illustration is that of the ass which in emulation of the dog fawned upon his master and was belabored for his pains.[32] To show how mercy multiplies riches the writer gives consecutively four short conventional exempla wherein mercy and charity are rewarded a hundred fold. They all tend to prove, as the holy man either intentionally or accidentally puts it, "þet merci is guod chapuare."[33] Besides these half-dozen unelaborated exempla and some negligible Biblical references there is only one other, somewhat longer than the rest. It is distinguished by the caption, "Hyer lyþ a tale." The illustration is a typical monkish legend of a hermit's fall from grace. A holy man once chanced to be in a temple of Mahomet. Here, surrounded by his cohorts, sat a chief devil. One after another the subordinates reported to their superior the diabolic havoc they had wrought in the way of wrecks, strife, discord, bloodshed, and murder, but one by one they were ordered to be flogged for sloth. At last spoke up one who after forty years of persistent effort had caused a holy man to commit fornication. Praise, kisses, embraces and a crown were awarded this devil by the ecstatic prince of darkness.[34] All these tales are told in 1340 substantially as they appeared some centuries previous. This emphasizes once more the fact that while the exemplum extended its scope, appeared in new combinations, and in some

---

[31] *Aȝenbite,* 45–6.

[32] *Ibid.,* 155–56.

[33] *Ibid.,* 191.

[34] *Ibid.,* 239–40. This tale with slight variations in detail and a vast difference in the manner of telling appears in the *Handlyng Synne* (pp. 246 seq.). Gaston Paris has pointed out that the tale is a composite from Gregory's *Dialogues* and the *Vitae Patrum.* Cf. *Hist. litt. de la France,* XXVIII, 201.

hands developed toward the short story, still in the main it retained its original form to the end of its flourishing period.

Probably Gower, who comes next in chronological order, made the most noteworthy attempt to turn the exemplum into secular channels, or better, to bring the secular tale into the ocean of exempla. But though the tales of the *Confessio Amantis* are given the semblance of moral illustrations, they far exceed the bounds of our type.

Gower's comprehensive vice and virtue treatise of thirty-one thousand lines, the *Miroir de l'Omme*,[35] prepared him for the *Confessio Amantis*. The tales in the former are comparatively few and brief, but of much significance when compared with those of the *Confessio*. Aside from the Biblical illustrations, we may note in the following list the marked tendency to exemplify observations by narratives of a secular tone:

> The envious man who would lose one eye in order that his comrade might lose two (Miroir, l. 3234)
> Socrates and his scolding wife (l. 4168)
> The robbery from the statue of Apollo (l. 7093)
> Lazarus and Dives (l. 7972)
> Ulysses and the sirens (l. 10909)
> Of the Emperor Valentinian (l. 17089)
> Of Sara, the daughter of Raguel (l. 17417)
> Of Phirinus who defaced his beauty (l. 18301)
> Of Codrus, King of Athens (l. 19981)
> Nebuchadnezzar's pride and fall (l. 21979)
> Of the king and his chamberlains (l. 22765)
> St. Macarius and the devil (two stories, ll. 12565, 20905)
> The undeserver relieved by St. Nicholas (l. 15757)
> The dishonest man who built a church (l. 15553)

All of these except the last four are found in expanded form in the *Confessio*.

In writing the *Confessio Amantis*, "Moral Gower" adapted the vice and virtue idea and even its terminology to the realm of love.[36] The exemplum had been successfully exploited in

---

[35] *The Complete Works of Gower*, ed. G. C. Macaulay. The *Miroir* and the *Speculum Meditantis* are identical.

[36] As Macaulay points out, this adaptation leads at times to amusing consequences; for example, "the moralist is found justifying unlawful love or the servant of Venus singing the praises of virginity."

these " miroir " treatises; it had been used with an increase of the secular tendency by Gower himself in the *Miroir de l'Omme*. With suggestions, perhaps, from the *Romance of the Rose* and other mediaeval productions he adopted this very convenient idea for bringing out his stories. Whereas mediaeval clerics had furnished a body of narratives fitted to moral and ecclesiastical rules and regulations, the poets and scholars had provided a fund of tales which were not badly adapted to illustrate an erotic structure. The latter form the body of the *Confessio*, while monkish stories are almost wholly absent. The melancholy king, how Boniface secured the papacy by deceit, Emperor Julius and the poor knight, the Pagan and the Jew, and a few historical and Biblical tales are all that in subject-matter resemble the exemplum.

In form, however, there is much to recall the type. The tales are uniformly introduced by a statement that Confessor is to tell a tale, or " ensample," of envy, pride, humility, or whatever vice or virtue of love is under discussion. The following passage dealing with the misuse of the eyes is typical:

> " Mi sone, herkne now forthi
> A tale, to be war therby
> Thin yhe forto kepe and warde,
> So that it passe noght his worde.
> Ovide telleth in his bok
> Ensample touchende of mislok."

This introduces the tale of Acteon, which is followed by the familiar restatement of the point involved:

> " Lo now, my sone what it is
> A man to caste his yhe amis,
> Which Acteon hath dere aboht;
> Be war forthi and do it noght."[37]

Moreover, the frequent use of the term " ensample " in the text and " exemplum " in the margin, together with frequent moral observations on the tales, serve as continual reminders of the type.

The exemplum, nevertheless, as I have intimated, loses its identity with Gower. The subject-matter of his tales is too

[37] *Conf. Amant.*, Bk. I, 44–6.

familiar to need recalling; they embrace a wide range of classic and mediaeval themes which were treated by such men as Boccaccio and Chaucer with little if any thought of the exemplum. To hold his tales together Gower used the exemplum idea instead of such a framework as that used in the *Decameron,* let us say. Such a notion was not altogether new, inasmuch as the *Dialogues* of Gregory follows much the same plan. Nor was the use of classic tales for illustrative purpose new, for Alfred, following Boethius, did the same thing in the *Consolation of Philosophy.* Still, a certain amount of credit must be allowed to Gower for bringing together the form of the exemplum with the matter of poetic narratives, and uniting them in a thorough-going fashion to the vices and virtues of love.

But after all is said, the real exemplum remains as before. Gower's stories of Apollonius, of Constance, and the others, are impressed soldiers in the army of erotic morality. They do battle much more bravely as free lances with Chaucer and Shakspere. The exemplum had acquired during its growth and spread a distinct character and a distinct setting. Gower may with the most laudable intentions tell long literary stories to illustrate his "miroir" of love, and may call them "exempla," but we who know Gregory, Valerius, Caesarius, and Jacques de Vitry, will term them merely "examples." They are at best exempla only by analogy.

Jacob's Well,[38] a comparatively little known treatise of the early part of the fifteenth century, brings us back to the real exemplum. The plan of the work combines in a consistent manner the free use of illustrative stories noted in the *Handlyng Synne* and the allegorical scheme of *Sawle Warde* or the *Abbey of the Holy Ghost.* A Biblical figure[39] is expanded into a truly marvelous allegory of the elaborate penitential scheme. A pit of oozy water and mire, representing man's body beset with sins, is to be made into a wholesome well wherein may flow the clear water of Divine Grace. The dirty water, or

[38] The date is probably the first quarter of the fifteenth century; see *Jacob's Well,* preface, xi.

[39] Cf. *John,* IV, 6.

Great Curse, must first be removed; then the mire, i. e., the seven deadly sins. Next the five water gates, the five senses, must be stopped up. After this the digging must continue until the seven pure springs, the gifts of the Holy Ghost, are reached. Then follows the walling process in which stones, sand, mortar, even the windlass, rope and bucket, are, needless to say, the customary virtues.

The work is based on a Latin original, but the Englishman, in adapting it for the farmers, merchants and artisans whom he addressed,[40] appears to have treated his source with something like the spirit of Robert of Brunne. These men, like Nicole de Bozon and others, were close to the people, knew their labors and amusements, their possibilities for good and their propensities to weakness, and discussed them in a simple, forcible, often broad manner.[41] It was this class of men who made most effective use of exempla.

At regular and frequent intervals *Jacob's Well* has a pair of exempla taken mainly from the *Vitae Patrum,* Jacques de Vitry, Caesarius, *Legenda Aurea,* and legends of the Virgin. The tales are therefore hackneyed, but they are frequently forged into a new glow by the striking diction of the zealous redactor.[42] To illustrate this point a few expressions from his typical narrative of the wicked clerk Odo may suffice. "þe feend dede hym be bathyd, & boyled, & sodyn, in pycche & oyle all sethyng over þe fyir." "He made hym be leyd on a bren-nyng grydell" and "rostyd wyþ brennyng bremston, wyþ blowyng under of belwes." "Whanne he was al for-rostyd, fryed, & scaldyd, & þus for-brent, he roryd as a devyl for peyne." Then the devil made him "drynke reed brennyng metal moltyn, til it ran out of his nose, eyȝin, & erys."[43] The writer customarily follows up such tales with dire threats of

[40] As Dr. Brandes points out, the ninety-five sections or chapters seem to have been delivered day by day as sermons, within the space of "þis hool tweyne monthys and more." Cf. *Jacob's Well,* preface, viii.

[41] Like Robert and Nicole, the writer of *Jacob's Well* does not shrink from the most indelicate terms or tales.

[42] This orthodox gentleman classes together "wycches, & heretykes, & Lollardys."

[43] *Jacob's Well,* 9 seq.

a similar fate to offending listeners. At the close of the tale just cited he says, "Þerfore, þou man & womman þat heryst þe word of god . . . be ware . . . for ʒif þou dyest wyth-oute repentauns, þou schalt be bathyd, as Ode was, in brennyng pycche & oyle! þou schalt be rostyd and fryed in þe fyir of helle! þou schalt drynken reed boylyng metal!" Of course the stories are uneven; some vivid, others dull; some brief, others elaborate. Though not so numerous, they are generally slightly longer than those in Mirk's *Festial*. Aside from the points noted, the previous discussion of Mirk's sermon collection applies to the present treatise.[44] With *Jacob's Well* the exemplum appears to have reached its maximum employment in the religious treatise, just as it did in sermon literature with the contemporary *Festial* of Mirk.

Before concluding this section on religious treatises I wish to speak of the *Myroure of Oure Ladye,* composed between 1408–50.[45] This work was evidently written by a scholar and was intended as an explanation of the divine service, the "hours" and "masses," not for a popular audience which needed to be entertained, but for the Sisters of Sion, a religious community near Isleworth on the Thames. The treatise is divided into three parts treating respectively of divine service in general, of the services for each day, of feasts and masses. The second and third parts, being rather technical expositions, did not lend themselves to illustration, but in the first part, which consists largely of general explanation and exhortation, encouragement of zeal and deprecation of neglect, exempla are freely used.[46]

The use of tales in this treatise differs somewhat from that in the popular ones. In the first place, a very restricted range of themes is represented. The benefits to be derived from praising Jesus and Mary, the evil of neglecting services, the wickedness of personal vanity in service, cover all of the narrative themes. Second, no suggestion of a new exemplum is

[44] See above, pp. 107 seq.

[45] *The Myroure of Oure Ladye,* preface, viii–ix. The editor, J. H. Blunt, with some probability inclines to the belief that the author was Dr. Thomas Gascoign of Merton College, Oxford.

[46] A few had appeared in the similar *Ancren Riwle;* see above, p. 88.

to be found; Cesarius and Gregory reign supreme. Third, the sixteen tales employed are not distributed with reference to points of weakening attention, but are used wherever occasion warranted and one or more apt illustrations were at hand. Finally, although even here the same absurdities still persist,[47] there is a notable absence of the personal, vivid quality which we noted in the more popular and sensational *Handlyng Synne* and *Jacob's Well*. Aside from these differences, the *Myroure* is noteworthy in showing that a scholar's dignified treatise for a more or less refined audience was not above the influence of the exemplum at the opening of the fifteenth century.

We may now review briefly the religious treatise before passing to the instruction-books. The exemplum was not universally employed in vernacular treatises; frequently, however, the allegorical structure was present where tales were lacking. In some cases both features were used. The exempla tended to expand in the works under discussion, but side by side with cases of expansion, the old example-book versions persisted. In the hands of Robert of Brunne the type approached in vivacity and originality of treatment the Chaucerian tale. Gower, in his *Miroir de l'Omme,* used, by the side of Biblical and monkish tales, a number of secular stories which, considering their brevity and their direct bearing upon moral issues, may be regarded as exempla in the technical sense. In the *Confessio Amantis* long secular narratives of a thoroughly literary character are given the office and concomitant features of exempla. In addition to this radical departure from tradition, the love setting, though couched in religious terminology, is foreign to the type; the exemplum therefore, loses its real identity in this work. *Jacob's Well* at the opening of the fifteenth century falls below *Handlyng Synne* in point of freshness of illustrative matter, but it has noteworthy vividness of expression and presents the most elaborate collection of favorite exempla of any treatise in this class. Finally, the

[47] The following themes are indicative: a monk saw a fiend gathering a sack full of high notes as they were sung (*Myroure,* 59); a holy man saw a fiend in the likeness of a little black boy leading a monk out of service (p. 31); the soul of a vain singer was snatched from his body by fiends (pp. 57–8).

10

Myroure of Oure Ladye with its conventional exempla indicates that the scholarly writer, even when addressing refined
audiences, found the type useful and not altogether beneath his
dignity.

The remaining class of writing with which exempla are
organically connected is the book of instruction. It must be
stated at the outset that illustrative tales play a relatively small
part in such treatises taken as a whole; nor is it to be wondered
at, since the exemplum was built up exclusively for moral and
religious purposes. One reads through treatise after treatise
of the usual courtesy-book type,[48] such as *A Book of Precedence, Stans Puer ad Mensam, The ABC of Aristotill, The
Babees' Book,* Hugh Rhodes' *Boke of Nurture,* John Russell's
Boke of Nurture without finding appreciable evidence of tales.
Naturally, exhortations not to pick the teeth at table nor
scratch the head in company did not give scope for illustrative
tales.

But a class of instruction-books developed which combined
features of the courtesy-book with those of the vice and virtue
treatise. Here the exemplum found a place. The original
of this class of works appears to be the *Secreta Secretorum,*[49]
a work supposed during the Middle Ages to have been written
by Aristotle at the request of Alexander. There are no
Greek texts extant but the work was transmitted through
Syriac to Arabic. From Arabic it was translated into Latin
by Johannes Hispalensis about the middle of the twelfth century. During the next century a second and enlarged Latin
translation was made by a Frenchman, Philip Tripolitanus.
From then on, the book spread widely over Europe,[50] and

[48] It does not seem advisable to enter upon a discussion of this type,
but the reader may be referred to the following essays: *Italian Courtesy
Books,* by W. M. Rossetti, printed in *E. E. T. S.* Ext. Ser., No. 8; *Early
German Courtesy Books,* by Eugene Oswald, printed in the same volume;
Edith Rickert's edition of the *Babees' Book* has a popular but suggestive
introduction.

[49] See Lydgate and Burgh's *Secrees of Old Philisoffres, a Version of
the Secreta Secretorum,* edited by Robert Steele for the *E. E. T. S.,*
Ext. Ser., No. 66. Cf. Warton, *op. cit.,* II, 312 seq.

[50] Steele has examined thirty MSS. in the British Museum alone and
suggests that there are doubtless others there. Spanish, Italian, and
French versions are extant.

served as the basis of a large number of treatises.[51] The
Secreta was obviously intended for the instruction of noble
persons, but in the explanations of the nature and effects of
precious stones, planets, fruits, wines, waters, physiognomy, the
care of the body and the development of character, there were
many things of more general application.

The work developed with little use of illustrative tales, but
two Englishmen in their rehandling of the treatise omitted
much of the encyclopædic matter, which did not invite narratives, and made exempla a notable feature. The first of
these was Thomas Hoccleve, whose poem, the *Regement of
Princes,* written in 1412, was based mainly on Egidio Colonna's
De Regimine Principum, some other version of the *Secreta
Secretorum,* the *Libellus de Ludo Scachorum* of Jacobus de
Cessolis, and an imposing list of other contributions to ancient
and mediaeval learning.[52] Hoccleve's work consists of two
parts: (1) a dialogue between Hoccleve and a beggar, in which
the social condition of contemporary England is depicted somewhat after the manner of *Piers Plowman;* (2) the "regement"
proper, in which are set forth for Prince Henry (later Henry
V) fifteen qualities befitting a man in high station.[53] The first
part has only a half dozen exempla,[54] but the second with its
discussion of noble qualities is copiously illustrated by tales.

The exempla, with the exception of a few Biblical nar-

[51] Prominent among these is Egidio Colonna's *De Regimine Principum;*
others are ascribed to Innocent III, Thomas Aquinas, Guillelmus Paraldus,
Simon Islip. Whether Giraldus Cambrensis' *De Principis Instructione* is
based upon the *Secreta* is doubtful; see Steele's forewords.

[52] Furnivall lists the sources cited by Hoccleve; see *Regement,* introd.,
xv–xvi.

[53] Such as justice, pity, mercy, patience, chastity, magnanimity.

[54] *Regement,* 41–2, 42–3, 46–7, 62–3. Near the close of the first section
Hoccleve says,

> "Of swiche stories cowde I telle an heepe,
> But I suppose þise schol suffice."

[55] Religious legends, such as that of the rich man who suddenly sank
into the earth with all his possessions (*Regement,* 46–7), are very rare.
Local anecdotes, such as that of the English king who pardoned a mur-
derer (*ibid.,* 113), are equally scarce.

ratives, are practically all[55] drawn from ancient history, particularly Roman, real or fabulous. A few typical themes may be cited: the return of Regulus to Carthage, the crucifiction of Theodorus for speaking the truth to a king, Camillus' refusal to deal with a traitor, the story of Phalaris' bull, Alexander's courtesy to a fallen knight.[56] Narratives of this kind were well adapted to illustrate such qualities as loyalty to one's oath, nobility of character, clemency, and similar social and civic virtues. The stories are told concisely, and in addition to their direct application to the points under discussion, they have unusual weight owing to the celebrity of the persons involved. Although the exempla are not as numerous as in Mirk's *Festial* or *Jacob's Well,* they are a prominent feature, and were used to excellent advantage in making the work interesting[57] and convincing to contemporary readers.

About 1420, James Young addressed to the Earl of Ormond,[58] Lord Deputy of Ireland, another English version of the *Secreta Secretorum,* in which he likewise introduced exempla. In his dedication of the work, which he called the *Governaunce of Prynces,*[59] he says, touching his additions, " I writte to your Excellence this boke, entremedelid wyth many good ensamplis of olde stories, and wyth the foure cardynale vertues, and dyvers othyr good matturis and olde ensamplis and new."[60] It is largely in connection with these "vertues

[56] *Regement,* 82, 93, 94–5–6, 109, 117–18, resp.

[57] The beggar says to Hoccleve just before the second section opens,

"Writte to hym [Prince Henry] a goodly tale or two,
On which he may desporten hym by nyghte,
And his fre grace schal up-on þe lighte."

[58] In his dedication, Young states that the Earl of Ormond had requested that there be translated "some good boke of governaunce of prynces out of latun othyr frenche in-to youre modyr tonge." *Regement,* 122.

[59] Steele, the editor, calls attention to a few later translations of the *Secreta* into English. Two of these, one from a French and one from a Latin source, are printed with Young's *Governaunce.* They are considerably abbreviated and contain no exempla worthy of note except two tales, the poison-maiden, and the Jew and the Mohammedan, both of which appear to be present in many early versions of the *Secreta Secretorum.* Cf. Lydgate and Burgh's *Secrees of Old Philisoffres,* introd., xiii.

[60] *Governaunce,* 123.

and dyvers othyr good matturis" that the exempla are used. The writer usually groups his tales instead of spreading them out as was the usual custom. After some discussion of a virtue he breaks off with a general heading under which he proceeds to narrate a number of tales. The following headings are typical: "Here folwyth ensamplis of olde stories to prow the forsayde lasson sothe," "Now here begynnyth olde stories to prowe the forsayde techynge of prudencia trowthe."[61] Under these captions are placed from four to six short narratives, frequently without paragraph division. In form and arrangement, therefore, the exempla present a considerable amount of irregularity.

In themes the illustrations in the *Governaunce* show two notable characteristics: the prominence of historical incidents, as was the case in the *Regement,* and the appearance of new narratives. To be sure, many of the historical exempla are taken from "the wyse clerke Valery" (Valerius), the *Bible* and the *Gesta Romanorum,* but historical works and modern events,[62] especially in Ireland, are also drawn upon. Young's confidence in new as well as old exempla is expressed as follows: "To prow that prayere hugely a-walyth agaynes the malice of enemys, dyvers good olde ensamplis abow in this boke y han writte; but for-als-moche as good newe ensamples sholde not ben unremembrid for lerynge of tho that arne to come, oone of tham now her y write."[63] He goes on in a page of his crude English to tell how the Dublin clergy, grieved by the Irish rebels, went twice a week in procession praying, with the result that Earl Butler overcame the enemy. Modern narratives of this sort, together with brief episodes from the wars of Alexander and Cyrus, the Trojan war, the life of Nero, Roman and Greek history, and a great number of mere historical references, are used to illustrate and confirm the writer's observations.

[61] *Governaunce,* 128, 149.

[62] *Ibid.,* 129, 133, 136, 182, 203–4. It will be remembered that in the example-books of Holkot, historical and classical narratives were especially prominent.

[63] *Ibid.,* 203.

The scarcity of the more strictly religious exempla is due to the character and purpose of the work. It was designed principally for the cultivation of persons of high rank, and in so far as it has more general application,[64] the tone is social rather than religious. The virtues, such as wisdom, prudence, fortitude and the like, which as I suggested above gave scope for illustrative tales, are not advocated as a means of escaping the "everlasting bonfire," but as making for uprightness, temporal felicity and success.

In these treatises of Hoccleve and Young we have secular narratives in greater prominence as exempla than we have hitherto noted. But though the tendency was to employ in instruction-books secular rather than religious tales, the latter were by no means excluded. This was due to the fact that a discussion of the ecclesiastical vices and virtues in some cases formed a part of the class under discussion. In that event the religious tale maintained a place beside the secular, as is exemplified in the *Book of the Knight of La Tour Landry*.

This work was completed in France in 1372 by Geoffrey de la Tour Landry[65] for his daughters.[66] "Je vouloye," he says, "faire un livre et un exemplaire pour mes filles aprandre à roumancier et etendre comment elles se doyvent gouverner et de bien du mal dessevrer."[67] During the reign of Henry VI the treatise was anonymously translated into English and found such favor that it was again translated by Caxton, who published it in 1484.

The author's statement concerning the compilation of the work is worthy of note. Realizing that "ancient stories" were excellent teachers, he engaged two priests and two clerks to extract for him "exempla from the Bible and other books that I had, as the acts of kings, the chronicles of France,

[64] Both Hoccleve and Young omitted most of the scientific and pseudo-scientific matter.

[65] On Geoffrey, see *Le Livre du Chevalier de la Tour Landry,* edited by Anatole de Montaiglon, preface, vi–xxvii. See also Wright's introduction to the *Book of the Knight of La Tour Landry.*

[66] Montaiglon points out that Geoffrey's book was not only for young girls but for the whole life of women. *Op. cit.,* preface, xxxiv.

[67] He says shortly after (*Le Livre,* 4) that he has made a similar book for his sons. This book has not been found.

Greece, England, and of many other strange lands."⁶⁸ The
resulting book is, in effect, a collection of classified tales. The
writer sets forth briefly the vices to be eschewed, interspersed
with the virtues to be emulated. These practically exhaust the
ecclesiastical list and include many other topics, such as the
desirability of women obeying their husbands, the evils which
result from over-familiarity with men, or excessive pride in
dress, and many similar points on the proper conduct of
women. The work is divided into one hundred and forty-four
chapters, each comprising a brief comment on some vice or
virtue and one or more entertaining tales in confirmation or
illustration. Above one hundred and fifty stories are used in
this way and constitute by far the greater part of the book.

It is the aim of the author to use only " profitable examples "
and not to speak as do some unworthy books "of love fables
and other worldly vanities."⁶⁹ Although the Knight has employed more Biblical tales than we have hitherto noted in any
treatise or set of sermons, his "profitable examples" include
an unusually large number of indelicate exempla. The pre-
vailing themes are those of the monkish legend, and the
fabliau so turned as to point a moral lesson. The tales about
Caesar, Alexander, and Camillus, which were employed in
books of princely culture, give way in this more popular
treatise to anecdotes of a more familiar nature, involving the
indiscretions and virtuous actions of ladies and knights in all
lands. Stories involving hermits, monks, saints, and miraculous happenings, are sufficiently numerous to preserve the
monastic flavor; these exempla employed by the Frenchman
differ in no respect from those with which we are already
familiar. Considering the tales of the *Book of the Knight* as
a body, they are strikingly similar in matter and form to those
of the *Gesta Romanorum* from which many are drawn, with
the same tendency to extend beyond the limits of exempla to
the scope and spirit of entertaining Boccaccian tales.

The foregoing works indicate the place and nature of
exempla in instruction treatises. Other books of a similar kind
show the same features, now favoring religious narratives and

⁶⁸ *Le Livre,* 4.
⁶⁹ *The Book of the Knight,* 118.

again those of secular tone. The *Liber Consolationis et Consilii* or *Instructions to his Son by Idle Peter of Kent* expands the *Stans Puer* theme and runs off into Biblical stories and tales from saints' lives.[70] The *Book of Cato*, after a long and varied career, takes unto itself monkish illustrations and a considerable number having more secular leanings, such as " An ensample of a cautele that a woman dyd to her husbond," " An ensample of a bawde and of her catte named Pasquette," " Of a quene that had a child by her cook."[71] The list of works might be extended but, as heretofore, to be exhaustive would be as impossible as valueless for our purpose. We may review briefly.

Since such topics as table manners, cookery, and cures for diseases did not permit illustration, the majority of instruction-books contain no narratives. But those treatises which aimed to inculcate civic and moral rectitude employed exempla constantly. Very frequently these works were adaptations of earlier productions and as was often the case in sermons and religious treatises, the tales were added to the originals. The vogue of exempla was so great by the end of the fourteenth century that they were interpolated with impunity into the most revered monuments of former days; wherever morals were discussed, our type was almost sure to be present. In books of princely instruction, historical themes are dominant; in the more popular treatises, monkish legends and fabliau themes morally turned are most prominent. The secular tone of the tales in the instruction-books is more marked than ever before,[72] and while the exempla as a class not only preserve their illustrative force but often appear in example-book form, their distinctness of character tends more and more to break down, as they merge with the great host of tales which were being told after the manner of Chaucer, Boccaccio, and the French *raconteurs*.[73]

[70] See *A Book of Precedence*, forewords, xxiii.

[71] See Dr. Max Otto Goldberg, *Die Catonischen Distichen während des Mittelalters in der engl. u. franz. Litteratur*. 53–6.

[72] The fable seems to have fallen largely into disuse as exemplum.

[73] Attention may be called to Professor H. V. Routh's suggestive remarks on the relation of exempla to jest-books, collections of *facetiae* and " mery tales." See *Camb. Hist. of Eng. Lit.*, III, 102 seq.

CHAPTER VI

Conclusion

Looking over the whole field we observe that while the exemplum played a considerable part in the early religious and didactic literature of England, it was distinctly an exotic feature, emanating largely from the Continental Church. Even the early traces of the type, before it became a factor in ecclesiastical literature, appeared as translations from Boethius and Gregory the Great. To the influence of these translations, together with their originals and the *Vitae Patrum,* may be ascribed almost wholly the use of exempla during the Old English period. Under such influence, legendary and Biblical illustrations attained considerable prominence in the discourses of Aelfric, but decreased in the *Wulfstan Homilies* and practically ceased in Old English sermons as the early influence died out.

During the eleventh and twelfth centuries, when vernacular preaching was at a low ebb, the scholars and clerics of England were circulating, collecting and employing in Latin compositions the monkish legends and fables then spreading among Continental churchmen. By the opening of the thirteenth century, therefore, Latin exempla were plentiful in England.

Even then it remained for the immigrant Dominicans and Franciscans to popularize the illustrative tale. Owing to the success which immediately resulted from their narrative method of preaching, collections began to appear in great numbers. England, as we have seen, made some compilations, but her monuments of this kind were few compared with those of Germany, France, or Italy; and in her greatest collections, the *Gesta Romanorum,* the *Speculum Laicorum,* Holkot's *Moralitates* and the *Liber Sapientiae,* and Bromyard's *Summa Praedicantium,* native tales are conspicuously few.

But by the opening of the fourteenth century these foreign

137

narratives had come to exert a powerful influence on religious composition. From then on into the fifteenth century the majority of popular preachers employed fables, anecdotes, and saints' legends in increasing numbers. Throughout the period, however, so far as may be judged by the extant literature, English preachers were fairly conservative in their use of tales. Undoubtedly there were numerous unrecorded cases of an extempore nature which go beyond John Mirk's tendency to abuse the narrative method. Wycliffe's outcries were probably based on abundant provocation. But in spite of opposition the exemplum thrived until the Reformation had aroused a more effective spirit of protest.

Following the use of exempla in sermons came their appearance in religious and didactic treatises. The religious treatises were composed of the same ecclesiastical instructions on righteous conduct which had formed a considerable part of the sermons. The fund of exempla was, therefore, equally adapted to the former. Here, the obvious limitations of the sermon were absent and exempla tended to expand and to assume the tone of literary narratives. Local color then became occasionally noticeable, though distinctive English characteristics were here, as elsewhere among the floating body of universal tales, sparse. In style, a marked advance beyond the exempla of the sermons appeared in the *Handlyng Synne;* and with Gower, entertaining secular tales in the guise of moral agents cannot be considered as exempla. But there was no general evolution; the religious treatise still preserved the old themes, excepting the fable, and in many cases the old manner. Departures from the traditional exemplum were, in general, only tendencies toward a merging with the great body of heterogeneous narratives.

Another step in the same direction characterized works of moral instruction after the opening of the fifteenth century. In those treatises which emphasize civic virtues, historical narratives appear in greater proportion than hitherto. When the instruction-book included the ecclesiastical vices and virtues, elaborated monastic legends were once more in evidence but, following the lead of France, fabliau themes with a moral *dénouement* appeared side by side with saints' legends and religious anecdotes.

So by the middle of the fifteenth century, while in sermons, religious and didactic treatises, the traditional monkish tale still appeared, an enormous variety of narratives had come into the class of exempla, which tended more and more to become entertaining stories rather than subordinate religious or moral agents.

At this point a new problem presents itself,—a more intensive study of the literary relations of the exemplum. The constant echoes of the type in the works of such men as Boccaccio and Chaucer, the specific abridgments of extended narratives for illustrative purposes, the corresponding expansion of exempla into independent literary productions, the exemplary poems, such as *The Wright's Chaste Wife, The Tale of the Incestuous Daughter, Dame Siriz, The Pennyworth of Wit or How a Merchant did his Wife Betray,*—all these matters invite a closer examination than was necessary or desirable in the foregoing pages. As far as was consistent with the work in hand I have attempted to show how exempla, narrated in the pulpit and at wayside gatherings, or brought together in collections, sermons, and treatises, originated or caught up and helped to popularize and perpetuate anecdotes, fables, apologues, fabliaux, *contes dévots,* saints' legends, and oriental tales. More particularly, the aim has been to examine the nature and development of exempla and to indicate the important part which they played in the religious and moral instruction of our credulous and story-loving ancestors.

LIST OF BOOKS CITED

No attempt is made in the following list to exhaust the sources consulted in the preparation of this study. For the convenience of the reader, the title and edition of the books cited in the foot-notes are given. All references to journals and periodical publications are sufficiently particularized in the notes.

Aelfric, *Homilies of the Anglo-Saxon Church,* ed. Thorpe, Aelfric Soc. Pub., 2 vols., London, 1844–46.

  Lives of Saints, ed. Skeat, E. E. T. S., 2 vols., Nos. 76–82, 94–114.

Alanus de Insulis, *Summa de Arte Praedicatoria,* ed. Migne, Patr. Lat., vol. CCX.

Aldhelm, *De Laudibus Virginitatis,* ed. Migne, Patr. Lat., vol. LXXXIX.

Alfred, *King Alfred's Old English Version of Boethius,* ed. Sedgefield, Oxford, 1899.

  King Alfred's Version of the Consolation of Boethius, translated into modern English by Sedgefield, Oxford, 1900.

  King Alfred's West-Saxon Version of Gregory's Pastoral Care, ed. with an English translation, Sweet, E. E. T. S., No. 45–50.

Alphabet of Tales, ed. Banks, E. E. T. S., Nos. 126, 127.

Altenglische Legenden, ed. Horstmann, Heilbronn, 1878.

Altenglische Legenden, Neue Folge, ed. Horstmann, Heilbronn, 1881.

Ancona, Alessandro d', *Studi di Critica e storia letteraria,* Bologna, 1880.

Ancren Riwle, ed. Morton, Camden Soc. Pub., London, 1853.

Anecdotes historiques, Légendes et Apologues tirées du Recueil inédit de Étienne de Bourbon, ed. Lecoy de la Marche, Paris, 1887.

Aubertin, C., *Histoire de la Langue et de la Littérature françaises au Moyen Âge,* 2 vols., Paris, 1883.

Babees' Book: Mediaeval Manners for the Young, ed. Rickert, New York and London, 1908.

Barlaam and Josaphat, ed. Jacobs, London, 1896.

Beda, *The Historical Works of Venerable Bede,* translated by Giles, 2 vols., 1843–45.

Bernard of Clairvaux, *Homiliae,* ed. Migne, Patr. Lat., vol. CLXXXIII.

Blickling Homilies, ed. Morris, E. E. T. S., No. 58–63–73.

Boethius, *Philosophiae Consolationis,* ed. Peiper, Leipzig, 1871.
The Consolation of Philosophy, translated by James, London, 1897.

Book of Precedence, ed. Furnivall, E. E. T. S., Ext. Ser., No. 8.

Bourgain, F. A., *La Chaire française au XIIᵉ Siècle,* Paris, 1879.

Bromya/d, John, *Summa Praedicantium,* 2 vols., Basel (undated).

Caesar of Heisterbach, *Dialogus Miraculorum,* ed. Strange, 1851.

Cambridge History of English Literature, ed. Ward and Waller.

Canby, H. S., *The Short Story in English,* New York, 1909.

Catalogi Veteres Librorum Ecclesiae Cathedralis Dunelm, pub. for the Surtees Society, London, 1838.

Catalogue of the Western Manuscripts in the Library of Emanuel College, compiled by James, Cambridge, 1904.

Caxton, *Golden Legend,* ed. Ellis, Temple Classics, 7 vols., 1900.

Courthope, W. J., *A History of English Poetry,* 6 vols., London, 1895–1910.

Cruel, R., *Geschichte der deutschen Predigt im Mittelalter,* Detmold, 1879.

Cursor Mundi, ed. Morris, E. E. T. S., Nos. 57, 59, 62, 66–68–69.

Cuthbert, Father, *The Friars and how they came to England,* London, 1903.

Dan Michel, *Aȝenbite of Inwyt,* ed. Morris, E. E. T. S., No. 23.

Dante, *The Divine Comedy,* trans., Cary.

Deutsche Predigten der XIII und XIV Jahrhunderten, ed. Leyser, *Bibl. der gesammt. deutsch. nat. Lit.,*

Dictionary of National Biography, ed. Stephen and Lee, 62 vols., New York and London, 1885–1900.

Douce, Francis, *Illustrations of Shakspere and of Ancient Manners,* 2 vols., London, 1807.

Dunlop, John, *The History of Fiction,* 2 vols., Philadelphia, 1842,

Earle, John, *Anglo-Saxon Literature,* London, 1884.

English Metrical Homilies, ed. Small, Edinburg, 1862.

Erasmus, *Stultitiae Laus,* Basel, 1780.

   Ecclesiastae sive de Ratione Concionandi, ed. Klein, Leipzig, 1820.

Förster, Max, *Über die Quellen von Aelfric's Homiliae Catholicae,* Berlin, 1892.

Freeman, E. A., *The History of the Norman Conquest of England,* 5 vols., Oxford, 1869–71.

Garnett, Richard, *A History of Italian Literature,* New York, 1898.

Gasquet, Abbot, *Parish Life in Mediaeval England,* London, 1907.

Gerould, G. H., *The North-English Homily Collection, a Study of the Manuscript Relations and the Sources of the Tales,* Lancaster, Pa., 1902.

Gervase of Tilbury, *Des Gervasius von Tilbury Otia Imperialia, in einer Auswahl neu herausgegeben,* Felix Liebrecht, Hannover, 1856.

Gesta Romanorum, ed. Madden, Roxburghe Club, 1838.

Gesta Romanorum, ed. Herrtage, E. E. T. S., Ext. Ser., No. 33.

Gesta Romanorum, ed. Oesterley, Berlin, 1872.

Gesta Romanorum, translated by Swan, New York, 1906.

Giraldus Cambrensis, *Giraldi Cambrensis Opera,* ed. Brewer, Dimock and Warner, Rolls Series, 8 vols., London, 1861–91.

Goldberg, Max Otto, *Catonischen Distichen während des Mittelalters in der engl. u. franz. Litteratur,* Leipzig, 1883.

Gower, *Works,* ed. Macaulay, 4 vols., Oxford, 1899–1902.

Green, J. R., *History of the English People,* 4 vols., New York, 1878–80.

Gregory the Great, *Homiliae in Evangelia,* ed, Migne, Patr. Lat., vol. LXXVI.

Dialogues, ed. Migne, Patr. Lat., vol. LXXVII.

Grein-Wülker, *Bibliothek der angelsächsischen Poesie,* 4 vols. in 3, Leipzig, 1883–98.

Bibliothek der angelsächsischen Prosa, 6 vols., Cassel, Hamburg, 1872–1907.

Hain, L., *Repertorium Bibliographicum,* 4 vols., Stuttgart, Paris and Tubingen, 1826–38.

Harnack, Adolph, *The History of Dogma,* trans., Buchanan, 7 vols., Boston, 1898–1903.

Harry, Philip, *A Comparative Study of the Aesopic Fable in Nicole Bozon,* Cincinnati University Studies, 1905.

Hervieux, Leopold, *Les Fabulistes Latins,* 5 vols., Paris, 1893–99.

Histoire littéraire de la France, 32 vols., Paris, 1832–98.

Hoccleve, Thomas, *The Regement of Princes,* ed. Furnivall, E. E. T. S., Ext. Ser., No. 72.

Holkot, Robert, *Super Libros Sapientiae,* Hagenau, 1494.

Jacob's Well, ed. Brandeis, E. E. T. S., No. 115.

Jacobus de Voragine, *Legenda Aurea,* ed. Graesse, Breslau, 1890.

Jacques de Vitry, *Exempla of Jacques de Vitry,* ed. Crane, Folk Lore Society Pub., vol. 26, London, 1890.

Jessop, Augustus, *The Coming of the Friars,* New York and London, 1889.

John of Salisbury, *Polycraticus,* ed. Migne, Patr. Lat., vol. CXCIX.

Julleville, L. Petit de, *Histoire de la Langue et de la Littérature française des Origines à 1900,* 8 vols., Paris, 1896–99.

Jusserand, J. J., *A Literary History of the English People,* 3 vols., London, 1895–1909.

English Wayfaring Life in the Middle Ages, trans., L. T. Smith, London, 1889.

Ker, W. P., *Essays on Mediaeval Literature,* London, 1905.

Kinard, J. P., *A Study of Wulfstan's Homilies,* Baltimore, 1897.

Körting, Gustav, *Grundriss der engl. Litteratur,* Münster, 1905.

Latimer, *Sermons by Hugh Latimer,* ed. Corrie, Parker Society Pub., vols. 16, 20.

Latin Stories, ed. Wright, Percy Society Pub., vol. VIII.

La Tour Landry, *Le Livre du Chevalier de la Tour Landry,* ed. Montaiglon, Paris, 1854.

La Tour Landry, *The Book of the Knight of La Tour Landry,* ed. Wright, E. E. T. S., No. 33.

Liber Exemplorum ad Usum Praedicantium, ed. Little, Society for Franciscan Studies, Aberdeen, 1908.

Lydgate and Burgh, *Secrees of Old Philisoffres, a Version of the Secreta Secretorum,* ed. Steele, E. E. T. S., Ext. Ser., No. 66.

Map, Walter, *Gualteri Mapes De Nugis Curialium,* ed. Wright, Camden Society Pub., London, 1850.

Marche, Lecoy de la, *La Chaire française au Moyen Age,* Paris, 1886.

Meray, Antony, *La Vie du Temps des libres Prêcheurs,* 2 vols., Paris, 1878.

Migne, J. P., *Patrologia Cursus Completus Latina.*

Miracles de la Sainte Vierge, traduit et mis en vers par Gautier de Coincy, ed. Pouquet, Paris, 1857.

Mirk, John, *Instructions for Parish Priests,* ed. Peacock, E. E. T. S., No. 31.

Festial, ed. Erbe, E. E. T. S., Ext. Ser., No. 96.

Monumenta Franciscana, ed. Brewer and Howlett, Rolls Series, 2 vols., London, 1858–82.

Myroure of Oure Ladye, ed. Blunt, E. E. T. S., Ext. Ser., No. 19.

Napier, A. S., *Über die Werke des altenglischen Erzbischofs Wulfstan,* Weimar, 1882.

Neckam, Alexander, *De Naturis Rerum,* ed. Wright, Rolls Series, London, 1863.

Nicole de Bozon, *Les Contes Moralizés,* ed. Paul Meyer and L. T. Smith, Société des Anciens Textes françaises, Paris, 1889.

Old English Homilies, ed. Morris, E. E. T. S., 2 vols., Nos. 29–34, 53.

Old English Miscellany, ed. Morris, E. E. T. S., No. 49.

Oliphant, T. L. Kington, *Old and Middle English,* London and New York, 1891.

Ormulum, ed. White, 2 vols., London, 1852.

Oswald, Eugene, *An Essay on Early German Courtesy Books,* E. E. T. S., Ext. Ser., No. 8.

Ott, J. H., *Über die Quellen der Heiligenleben in Aelfric's Lives of Saints,* Halle, 1892.

Paris, Gaston, *La Littérature française au Moyen Âge,* Paris, 1905.

Paul, Hermann, *Grundriss der germanischen Philologie,* 3 vols., Strassburg, 1891–1900.

Religious Pieces in Prose and Verse, ed. Perry, E. E. T. S., No. 26.

Robert of Brunne, *Handlyng Synne, with the French treatise on which it was founded, Le Manuel des Pechiez by William of Wadington,* ed. Furnivall, Roxburghe Club, 1862; re-ed. Furnivall, E. E. T. S., No. 119–23.

Robinson, J. H., *Petrarch, the First Modern Scholar and Man of Letters,* New York, 1898.

Rolle, Richard, *English Prose Treatises of Richard Rolle de Hampole,* ed. Perry, E. E. T. S., No. 20.

  Pricke of Conscience, ed. Morris, Philological Society, Berlin, 1863.

  Richard Rolle of Hampole and his Followers, ed. Horstmann, 2 vols., London, 1895–96.

Rossetti, W. M., *An Essay on Italian Courtesy Books,* E. E. T. S., Ext. Ser., No. 8.

Saint Dunstan, *Memorials of Saint Dunstan, Archbishop of Canterbury,* ed. Stubbs, Rolls Series, vol. 63.

Saint Juliana, Life of, ed. Cockayne, E. E. T. S., No. 51.

Saint Katherine, Life of, ed. Einenkel, E. E. T. S., No. 81.

Saint Margaret, Life of, ed. Cockayne, E. E. T. S., No. 13.

Sarrazin, Gregor, *Über die Quellen des Orrmulum,* Altenburg, 1882.

Scherer, W., *A History of German Literature,* trans., Conybeare, 2 vols., New York, 1906.

Schofield, W. H., *English Literature from the Norman Conquest to Chaucer,* New York, 1906.

Secreta Secretorum, Three Prose Versions of the Secreta Secretorum, ed. Steele, E. E. T. S., Ext. Ser., No. 74.

Snell, F. J., *The Age of Transition,* 2 vols., London, 1905.

11

South English Legendary, ed. Horstmann, E. E. T. S., No. 87.

Stevenson, F. S., *Robert Grosseteste, Bishop of Lincoln,* London, 1899.

Taylor, H. O., *The Classical Heritage of the Middle Ages,* New York, 1901.

Ten Brink, Bernard, *History of English Literature,* trans., Kennedy, Robinson and Schmitz, 3 vols., New York, 1889–96.

Traill, H. D., *Social England,* 6 vols., New York and London, 1893–97.

Tupper, J. W., *Tropes and Figures in Anglo-Saxon Prose,* Baltimore, 1897.

Vices and Virtues, ed. Holthausen, E. E. T. S., No. 89.

Vitae Patrum, ed. Migne, *Patr. Lat.,* vol. LXXIII.

Vollhardt, W., *Einfluss der lateinischen geistlichen Litteratur auf einige kleinere Schöpfungen der englischen Übergangsperiode,* Leipzig, 1888.

Ward, H. L. D., *Catalogue of the Romances in the Department of Manuscripts of the British Museum,* 2 vols., London, 1883–93.

Warton, Thomas, *The History of English Poetry,* 4 vols., London, 1824.

Werferth, *Dialoge Gregors,* ed. Grein–Wülker, *Bibliothek der angelsächsischen Prosa,* vol. V.

White, C. L., *Aelfric. A New Study of his Life and Writings,* Yale Studies in English, 1898.

William of Wadington, *Manuel des Pechiez.* (See Robert of Brunne.)

Wordsworth, C., and H. Littlehales, *The Old Service Books of the English Church,* London, 1904.

Wright, Thomas, *Biographia Britannica Literaria,* 2 vols., London, 1846.

Wulfstan; Sammlung der ihm zugeschriebenen Homilien nebst Untersuchungen über ihre Echtheit, ed. Napier, Berlin, 1883.

Wycliffe, *The English Works of Wycliffe,* ed. Matthew, E. E. T. S., No. 74.

Young, James, *The Governaunce of Prynces,* ed. Steele, E. E. T. S., Ext. Ser., No. 74.

INDEX

147

THE COLUMBIA UNIVERSITY PRESS

STUDIES IN ENGLISH

Joseph Glanvill. By FERRIS GREENSLET, Ph.D., Cloth, 12mo, pp. xi + 235, $1.50 *net*.

The Elizabethan Lyric. By JOHN ERSKINE, Ph.D., Cloth, 12mo, pp. xvi + 344, $1.50 *net*.

Classical Echoes in Tennyson. By WILFRED P. MUSTARD, Ph.D., Cloth, 12mo, pp. xvi + 164, $1.25 *net*.

Sir Walter Scott as a Critic of Literature. By MARGARET BALL, Ph.D., Paper, 8vo, pp. x + 188, $1.00 *net*.

The Early American Novel. By LILLIE DEMING LOSHE, Ph.D., Paper, 8vo, pp. vii + 131, $1.00 *net*.

Studies in New England Transcendentalism. By HAROLD C. GODDARD, Ph.D., Paper, 8vo, pp. x + 217, $1.00 *net*.

A Study of Shelley's Drama "The Cenci." By ERNEST SUTHERLAND BATES, Ph.D., Paper, 8vo, pp. ix + 103, $1.00 *net*.

Verse Satire in England before the Renaissance. By SAMUEL MARION TUCKER, Ph.D., Paper, 8vo, pp. xi + 245, $1.00 *net*.

The Accusative with Infinitive and Some Kindred Constructions in English. By JACOB ZEITLIN, Ph.D., Paper, 8vo, pp. viii + 177, $1.00 *net*.

Government Regulation of the Elizabethan Drama. By VIRGINIA CROCHERON GILDERSLEEVE, Ph.D., Cloth, 8vo, pp. vii + 259, $1.25 *net*.

The Stage History of Shakespeare's King Richard the Third. By ALICE I. PERRY WOOD, Ph.D., Cloth, 8vo, pp. xi + 186, $1.25 *net*.

The Shaksperian Stage. By VICTOR E. ALBRIGHT, Ph.D., Cloth, 8vo, pp. xii + 194, $1.50 *net*.

Thomas Carlyle as a Critic of Literature. By FREDERICK W. ROE, Ph.D., Cloth, 8vo, pp. xi + 152, $1.25 *net*.

The Authorship of Timon of Athens. By ERNEST HUNTER WRIGHT, Ph.D., Cloth, 8vo, pp. ix + 104, $1.25 *net*.

English Tragicomedy, Its Origin and History. By FRANK H. RISTINE, Ph.D., Cloth, 8vo, pp. xv + 247, $1.50 *net*.

Lemcke & Buechner, Agents

30-32 West 27th Street   **New York**

STUDIES IN ENGLISH

Leigh Hunt's Relations with Byron, Shelley and Keats. By BARNETTE MILLER, Ph.D. 8vo, cloth, pp. vii + 169, $1.25 net.

The Rise of the Novel of Manners. By CHARLOTTE E. MORGAN, Ph.D. 8vo, cloth, pp. ix + 271. Price, $1.50 net.

John Dennis. His Life and Criticism. By HARRY G. PAUL, Ph.D. 8vo, cloth, pp. viii + 229. Price, $1.25 net.

The Political Prophecy in England. By RUPERT TAYLOR, Ph.D. 8vo, cloth, pp. xx + 165. Price, $1.25 net.

New Poems of James I. of England. By ALLAN F. WESTCOTT, Ph.D. 8vo, cloth. Price, $150 net.

The Middle English Penitential Lyric. By FRANK ALLEN PATTERSON, Ph.D. 8vo, cloth. Price, $1.50 net.

The Exemplum in the Early Religious and Didactic Literature of England. By JOSEPH ALBERT MOSHER, Ph.D. 8vo, cloth. Price, $1.25 net.

The Soliloquies of Shakespeare. By MORRIS LEROY ARNOLD, Ph.D. 8vo, cloth. Mathew Carey, Editor, Author and Publisher. By EARL L. BRADSHER, Ph.D. 8vo, cloth. Price, $1.25 net.

Thomas Dekker. A Study. By MARY LELAND HUNT, Ph.D. 8vo, cloth. Price, $1.25 net.

STUDIES IN COMPARATIVE LITERATURE

Romances of Roguery. By FRANK WADLEIGH CHANDLER, Ph.D. Part I. The Picaresque Novel in Spain. 12mo, cloth, pp. ix + 483. Price, $2.00 net.

A History of Literary Criticism in the Renaissance. By JOEL ELIAS SPINGARN, Ph.D. Second edition, revised and augmented. 12mo, cloth, pp. xi + 330. Price, $1.50 net.

Platonism in English Poetry of the Sixteenth and Seventeenth Centuries. By JOHN SMITH HARRISON, Ph.D. 12mo, cloth, pp. xi + 235. Price, $2.00 net.

Irish Life in Irish Fiction. By HORATIO SHEAFE KRANS, Ph.D. 12mo, cloth, pp. vii + 338. Price, $1.50 net.

The English Heroic Play. By LEWIS NATHANIEL CHASE, Ph.D. 12mo, cloth, pp. xii + 250. Price, $2.00 net.

The Oriental Tale in England in the Eighteenth Century. By MARTHA PIKE CONANT, Ph.D. 12mo, cloth, pp. xxvi + 312. Price, $2.00 net.

The French Influence in English Literature. By ALFRED HORATIO UPHAM, Ph.D. 12mo, cloth, pp. ix + 560. Price, $2.00 net.

The Influence of Molière on Restoration Comedy. By DUDLEY H. MILES, Ph.D. 12mo, cloth, pp. xi + 272. Price, $1.50 net.

The Greek Romances in Elizabethan Prose Fiction. By SAMUEL LEE WOLFF, Ph.D. 12mo, cloth. Price, $1.50 net.

Lemcke & Buechner, Agents,

30–32 West 27th Street   New York